the
Legal & Moral Rights
of All Artists

the
Legal & Moral Rights of All Artists

Amelia V. Vetrone

iUniverse, Inc.

New York Lincoln Shanghai

the Legal & Moral Rights of All Artists

iUniverse, Inc.

For information address:
iUniverse, Inc.
2021 Pine Lake Road, Suite 100
Lincoln, NE 68512
www.iuniverse.com

Cover Design by Dzn Duo, Inc.

The purpose of this book is to provide a general knowledge of legal concepts to non-lawyers who will encounter these issues in the marketplace of artistic works. It should not be construed as complete legal advice for any specific situation which the reader may be experiencing. It is not a substitute for the legal advice of an experienced attorney who may provide one-on-one attention and a thorough analysis of the facts involved in a particular scenario, and the reader is encouraged to seek such advice.
In other words, don't sue me.

ISBN: 0-595-29683-1 (pbk)
ISBN: 0-595-66035-5 (cloth)

Printed in the United States of America

To my Mentor, Daisaku Ikeda

Contents

Part III   What Can Be Done

Acknowledgements

There are a lot of people I need to thank for the assistance and support I've needed to see this book through to publication. First of all, I thank Elaine Hui for her solid commitment and support for my efforts in writing this book, and a big kiss to Steve Edwards, who has seen me through the ups and downs of this crusade with love, compassion and understanding. Thanks to Mike Altman at iUniverse for his help with this book. For their experience, insight, and patience in talking with me I thank some brilliant legal minds in the field of art law: Leonard DuBoff, Peter Karlen, John Merryman, Ken Norwick and Hamish Sandison. To the artists who have not allowed me to give up on this book, I thank the Artists Rights Foundation (especially Gene Reynolds and Elliot Silverstein), Sunny Bak, Bobbi Bennett, Mick Curran, Ed Freeman, Emma Hayashida, Katherine Lam, Karen Quincy Loberg, Will Prosser, Denise Railla, Julian Semilion, Jerry Threadgill and Joyce Weatherford. For the moral support that has sustained me since I began this project more than twelve years ago I thank Kyla Chambers, Susan Chambliss, Tony Cohan, Val Crawford, Donna Darnell, Margaret Leslie Davis, Irena Dragustinovich, Yvette Edmond, Steve Elias, Mayke Han, Kay Haugaard, Jonathan Kirsch, Kathy Kozak, the regulars at News Junkie Café, Jim Norris, George Odano, Janet and Tom Sexton, T. Fitzgerald Smith, Bruce and Connie Stratton, and, of course, my parents Fernando Vetrone and Grace Hubbell, who continually asked when my book was coming out. I also have to thank the staffs of Buster's Ice Cream and Coffee Stop in South Pasadena and Green Street East Restaurant in Pasadena, California for providing me with hospitable places to spread out and work when I needed to be alone. For their editing assistance I thank Donna Hinton, Andrew Hubbell and Carmen Silva. Finally, I have to thank a few literary agents who gave me their time and some very valuable advice, even though they didn't represent me: Charlotte Gusay, Laura Langlie, and Mike Larsen.

Introduction

Another thing that interested us enormously was how different the camouflage of the french looked from the camouflage of the germans, and then once we came across some very very neat camouflage and it was american. The idea was the same but as after all it was different nationalities who did it the difference was inevitable. The colour schemes were different, the designs were different, the way of placing them was different, it made plain the whole theory of art and its inevitability.

—Gertrude Stein,
The Autobiography of Alice B. Toklas

I grew up in the middle of America. I was taught to work hard and learn what I needed to know to get a respectable job and make a nice living. Art was a fun, spare time activity. In high school, the art class studios were in a remote corner of the building next to the large room where the band practiced. The art students were weird. Then I graduated from high school and left my small hometown for the first time. I traveled to Italy to visit my paternal grandparents, and I saw what the world looks like when art is an integral part of every aspect of life, and not merely a hobby.

As a senior in college I returned to Europe for a year-long study abroad in England. I traveled extensively, and flourished in an environment that accorded me a certain basic level of dignity, even as a penniless student, carrying all my belongings in a backpack. As a penniless student in the United States of America I had not received such respect. When I returned to Los Angeles, I bristled at the coarseness of my surroundings and tried to figure out why. As a second year law student I stumbled upon an article about artistic moral rights and I knew I had found an answer.

The difference in the regard for art and artists mirrored the regard for basic human dignity and individuality that I had experienced in Europe. The extensive legal protection for artists in other countries reflected a formal, official recognition of that reality. We needed to treat our artists better and, in doing so, we would treat each other better and enhance the beauty of our world.

I studied the laws this country had to protect artists and learned that those laws had nothing whatsoever to do with art. They protected the owner of the art, the owner's rights to make money with the art, and—I was shocked to learn—the owner's rights to make changes to the art.

Art is perceived as a product of culture and the history of society. It defines the origins and progress of a people. To revise, censor or "improve" a work of art, then, is in a sense to falsify that culture. If Humphrey Bogart can be made to look as though he is sharing a soft drink with a modern actor in a television commercial, what can John F. Kennedy, or Martin Luther King, Jr., or Michelangelo's "David" be made to do? Although these portrayals are usually comic, they chip away at the feelings we experience when we view the unaltered original work of art. Such activity separates us from the reaction we would naturally have to the work on our own, thereby separating us from our own conscience, our own instincts, in short, ourselves. It is this, not the art, that is sacred.

People the world over will endure endless lines to view the honest and unfiltered expressions of artists in museums and galleries. When Fred Rogers retired he was asked for his opinion on the enduring popularity of the television program, "Mr. Rogers' Neighborhood." He replied that people yearn for honesty, and his primary goal on the show was to give it to them. Joseph Campbell, in "The Power of Myth," observed that artists are gifted people whose ears are open to the song of the universe. The ability to perceive the artist's expression, as the artist intended, enables us to hear that song and be reassured in our innate wisdom. With that song in our ears we can't be deceived. If people change their views about art, they will change their views about life.

PART I

Beyond the Price Tag—The Notion of Artists' Rights

1

The Problem

Last year, recording artists Don Henley and Alanis Morissette pleaded with members of the United States Senate to allow artists to be included in the decisions regarding the passage of laws that regulate their creative output. As the Senate Judiciary Committee considered ways to amend the copyright laws to govern distribution of artistic works on the Internet, the artists composed two of a ten-member panel. The rest of the seats were occupied by representatives from the motion picture, music, and television industries.

The hearings were sparked by the Internet phenomenon called "Napster," which enabled millions of young people to download music from the Internet for free until court action shut it down. This experience raised public awareness of the laws that regulate artistic works, namely copyright laws, and illustrated the broad effect such laws have on the lives of consumers who want access to the works they enjoy.

While most people believe that copyright laws protect artists and their works, the disappointing reality is that creative people, no matter how famous, have virtually no control over what happens to their works once they have been paid. They are not automatically protected as the people who originally created the works. Our legal framework actually has no provisions for recognizing the artist's role in creating the work, even though the public is responding to the artist when they respond to the work.

Art functions as a unifying force. In those moments when we are touched by some form of creative expression—a song, a photograph, a mural, a perfectly-thrown touchdown pass—we understand, for an instant, what life is all about. We arrive at a moment of truth generated by our own innate wisdom, and that truth stays with us, even when we are no longer aware of it. Art is the only thing created by humans that can communicate so powerfully and honestly to the point of transformation. That is why it is worth protecting.

When a work of art has been altered or edited from its original form, it loses its power. The public does not have the opportunity to be moved by the art's message, and the artist does not have the opportunity to gain recognition as a talented artist. Yet this activity takes place in the United States of America all the time. People who own art change it, just because they can. Usually they do it to make money with the art, but changing a work of art doesn't necessarily make it more profitable. Sometimes the opposite effect is realized, such as the public's distaste for colorized movies.

Most people believe that great works of art are preserved in museums or archives and that mutilating art is against the law. In reality, the United States provides a smaller amount of funding for museums and other arts-related endeavors than any other industrialized nation in the world. And although 150 countries around the world have laws to protect and preserve works of art, the United States has virtually none.

That means that almost all created works in this country are owned or controlled by private hands who, by law, can do whatever they want with, or to, these works. In other countries throughout the world, artists can protect their creative expression, even if they no longer own it. In this country, they must stand idly by as commercial owners of their works cut, color, crop, sample or otherwise misrepresent the original creative expression.

Art, when it is created, is honest. It tells us so much and gives us so much. If the people who own it have the right to change it, they can make the art say what they want it to. They can change what the artist has tried to communicate into something they think people should see and hear. The commercial interests of others do not belong inside us. Someone who has the money to buy the copyright to your favorite film, store the original master version of it and reproduce it on video-tape or DVD, should not have the power to alter that film when the artists who created it have no power to protect it. But that is the way it is right now. All other developed nations in the world regard art and artists as beneficial contributors to society, worthy of legal protection. In this country, art and artists are treated by the law as products to be bought and sold. That's not good for anyone. The creative expression that has emanated from a person's heart should not be reduced to a bottom line and given access to the public only in the form that the person paying for that access allows.

Artists, when they can, avoid allowing others to control their expression. For example, after Jonathan Winters retired, he performed comedy in his local market. A family member asked him why he would rather perform for a few people for free than in an auditorium for many people and get paid thousands of dollars. His answer was that, in the market, he could perform comedy on his own terms.

People want to know what the artist has to say. That is why art museums all over the world—such as the Louvre, in Paris, France—endure endless lines of people from all walks of life who wait to see expressions of fine art exhibited in their original forms. The expressions are honest and unfiltered and people can't get enough of that.

There's something more. Having respect for the creative expression of another person is also respect for the dignity and individuality of that person. A person does not derive their entitlement to respect from another person's willingness to invest money in them. A person's ideas are not better or more valid because someone has gone to the expense to disseminate them widely. Right now that is where the law goes. Because it is much easier to measure and to define, our laws follow the money and the point of view that has attracted the money is the one the law protects. That's why our laws of copyright protect the owner of a work of art, or the owner of the rights to make money with the art. Moral rights, sometimes called *droit moral,* are laws that protect the artist's right to stand up for the expression he or she created, or for the reputation the artist has to protect by making sure the public sees the work of art as it was originally intended.

Laws reflect the thinking of the society that passes them. Our laws reflect the thinking that the person most entitled to legal protection with regard to art is the person who owns or has the rights to make money with it. By recognizing moral rights laws, the work itself is given legal protection, in addition to the protections given to its owners. The message that the artist is trying to communicate is just as important as the money used to bring it to the public and the law protects both, when it is followed. Having access to original works of art is good for us as a society as well. Original works of art point us to our own inner truths, and those truths will set us free.

2

History of Legal Protection for Artists

The historical development of artists' rights protection explains the modern manifestations of such protection in such cases as Napster and the "Winnie the Pooh" decision issued earlier this year by the United States Supreme Court.

Ancient Greece and the Roman Empire

When most people think about a creator's legal rights, they think about copyright law. But, as one legal scholar has observed, "copyright" addresses the natural needs of the body for food in order to sustain physical development, while other rights—such as moral rights—address the needs of the mind in order to sustain mental development.[1] These other rights—much older than copyright—are much broader, and the extent of their protection of art and artists is found in history.

Under the Ancient Greek system, the rights of creative people were part of the doctrine of natural law. The recognition of natural law began with ancient philosophers, such as Aristotle and the Stoics, who taught that a universal working force pervades everything, creating a natural justice that is valid everywhere, with the same force and effect for all people.[2] The philosophers, on this basis, advocated that human behavior should be brought into harmony with nature in order for people to receive the benefits and protection of that law. It was originally intended that governmental laws were nothing more than formal

11

recitations of rights that already existed and flowed from the human experience.

In Ancient Greece, also known as the Golden Age of Greece, all people enjoyed the full legal protection of their natural rights. One of the natural rights recognized by the Ancient Greeks concerned what we now regard as "plagiarism." It was known by the term "plagium," defined as "the crime of stealing a human being." There is one documented example of the enforcement of a creator's rights under that early system. Following a literary contest in Alexandria during the reign of one of the Ptolemies, Aristophanes the Grammarian (c. 257–180 B.C.), acting as judge, selected as the winner a contestant whose composition was not the best entry, but it was original. The other contestants' productions were literal copies from the works of authors well known at the time. The unsuccessful contestants were promptly brought before the local court, sentenced as thieves, and thrust out of the city.[3]

When the Romans conquered Greece in about 146 B.C., they developed a great admiration for the literature of the Greek writers. The demand for it was so high that the task of publishers became quite daunting. Specially trained and educated slaves, called "scribes," were employed to hand write copies of the original texts on Egyptian papyrus for distribution and sale to the public. The author of the original manuscript supervised the publishing process to ensure the accuracy and quality of the reproductions. The entire process was very slow, by today's standards.

Because of the overwhelming demand for these works, many publishers cut corners by dispensing with the thorough training of the scribes in order to be able to produce the books more rapidly. However, due to their lack of training the second-rate scribes made many mistakes. The sloppy and inaccurate texts were distasteful to the reading public who apparently went well out of their way to obtain true reproductions and referred to the substandard material as "libri mendosi," or "books that lie."[4]

Although the Ancient Greek and Roman authors achieved fame through their works and exerted almost complete control over maintaining the accuracy of reproductions, it was concluded by Putnam that book authors did not write for money. Authors were paid for publicly reciting their works, which they alone did, but Putnam surmised that it was the prestige of authorship that attracted them. On the other hand, playwrights were handsomely paid for their creations, and composers were paid for their performances.[5]

The Middle Ages

Following the fall of the Roman Empire in about 410, the Western world busied itself with widespread war for approximately 1000 years. This period is known alternately as the Middle Ages or the Dark Ages. During the Middle Ages, the doctrine of natural law became confused with the term "the laws of nature," relied upon by sovereigns to assert their authority as being derived from God and nature. Heavy emphasis was placed on the "duties" as opposed to the "rights" of people, and natural law was used to support and justify the regime in power. Such justification was akin to Darwinian theory and supported the belief that those in positions of power were there because they were naturally selected for it.[6]

The creation and maintenance of artistic works was found mainly in the Roman Catholic Church until approximately the fourteenth century. The Church is generally recognized as the entity that for over six hundred years preserved the scholastic and literary heritage of Greece and Rome for modern civilization.

While the Church proscribed plagiarism, it tried to exert monopolistic control over the content of created works. It encouraged monks to copy and transcribe "good" books. Paintings and sculpture were created for the purpose of adorning churches, monasteries, and residences of high-level church officials. Even music was intended for use in worship services. A class of music known as "plainsong," or "plain chant," was developed during this period. The concept of individual recognition with respect to art was unknown during this period, although the chant which was developed during the papacy of Gregory I is now described as the "Gregorian Chant." All ownership of works created in Europe was lodged firmly in the Church, with the exception of what was then known as "profane music," the performances of the minstrels.[7]

The Minstrels (Poet-musicians), took it upon themselves to preserve the profane (non-sacred) music, secular traditions, ancient laws, and legendary exploits of the past and the then-present. The Minstrels were lineal descendants of pagan poet-musicians and were influenced by the actors of the late Roman theatre. These performers were considered outcasts under the Roman law because they "devoted themselves to various activities—frequently of a dubious nature—among which was the playing of instruments."[8] The church and the state issued numerous edicts to try to control their behavior, but their popularity kept them thriving. Even after the minstrels were organized into recognized guilds early in the 12th century, individual artists were not regarded as creators, or owners, of the works they performed.

At the beginning of the 13th century, the responsibility for the preservation and development of intellectual property in Western Europe was transferred from the monasteries and ecclesiastical schools to the newly organized universities, where church scholars taught. For the first time, private citizens, albeit university students, were allowed to own copies of books previously owned and maintained by the Church. The institution of book manufacturing for the purpose of making student copies led to a broader production of secular books for the general public.

The lessening of Church control and censorship during this period was the prologue for the freedom and expression of the new ideas of the Renaissance: the dawn of enlightenment. The Renaissance was the beginning of individual recognition of artists for their works, as well as the ability of artists to create works that they themselves wanted to produce.

The Renaissance through the Statute of Anne

Italy must be viewed as the birthplace of this great movement and Florence as it's focal point. Like moths to a flame, scholars, philosophers, authors and artists from all over flocked to the court of the Medicis for patronage, protection and prestige.[9] Art flourished and the people enjoyed a culture that supported artists such as Michelangelo, Leonardo da Vinci, and Botticelli. It was also the rebirth of the recognition of the doctrine of natural law and the philosophy of humanism.

The Renaissance opened the minds of people to the freedoms to create, to engage in philosophical debate, and to study. However, the event that had the greatest impact on changing everyday life was the invention of the printing press. Most authorities agree that the printing press was invented by Johann Gutenberg in about 1440, and the evidence of his invention is found in legal records. His financial backer, who had loaned Gutenberg the money to make his press, foreclosed on the loan and took possession of the press. The accounting of the items foreclosed set forth the press and type for a 42 line Bible and Psalter.[10]

At first the Church welcomed the convenience of the printing press, but after the publication of works by Luther, and others who challenged the Church's authority and doctrines, it realized that the printing press was a dangerous thing. The Church engaged in a campaign of censorship and repression to control printing, but all its efforts failed to put the cat back into the bag. Due to the preoccupation of both France and England with the Hundred Years War until 1453, the division between the Christians and the Moors in Spain, and indeterminate petty wars among the German, Scandinavian and Slavic states, the influence of the Renaissance was late in arriving in the rest of western Europe. When it did, however, it combined with the Reformation and the printing press effectively to curtail the final vestige of control of created works which the Church had exercised by default since the fall of Rome.[11]

The sovereign rulers of Europe, having learned from the mistakes of the Roman Church, moved quickly to control the printing of everything to avoid the circulation of material that could be considered heretical or seditious. It is from these acts that the modern laws governing products of the mind—intellectual property—are derived.

Although each country had similar requirements that all printers be authorized by the ruling authority to engage in the activity of printing, the most documented history of this practice is found in England. Queen Mary I of England granted a charter for an agency to oversee the publication of all reading matter to the now famous Stationers' Company of England in 1557.[12]

Under its charter, the Stationers' Company granted all licenses to print books in England and its possessions, and only members of the Stationers' Company were granted such licenses. In the event of any conflict over publishing rights, the dispute was handled under the Stationers' authority by an arbitering body known as the "Star Chamber."

As a result of this censorship by the State, the businessmen of the Stationers' Company directly benefited monetarily by controlling and regulating the entire English book trade, from printing to sale. To say, however, that no authors' rights existed during the Stationers' period is too broad. Despite the fact that during the Elizabethan period authors were held in low esteem and had to rely on patrons for support until the eighteenth century, there are recorded occasions of the grant of a Stationers' license to an author for his works. In addition, the Stationers' indirectly recognized the author's creative rights which included, though unarticulated, his moral rights.[13]

Although the Stationers' system was fraught with problems, the one aspect of it that motivated significant change by the government was the fact that the Stationers' right did not expire. In other words, once the Stationers' Company granted a license to a publisher to publish a book, that license lasted forever. This restraint of the book trade was perceived as unfair, and resulted in the passage of the law which is considered the foundation of modern American copyright law: the Statute of Anne.

For the first time since Ancient Rome, the rights to created works—in this case books—were recognized to reside in the person of the author. The original right to publish was established as belonging to the author, and thereafter to any and all persons holding through the author. The other significant change encoded in the Statute of Anne was the placing of time limits on exclusive rights to publish. At the expiration of the stated time periods the works would pass into the public domain, meaning that no person had any exclusive rights in them whatsoever.

The Statute of Anne created "copyright" and separated it in legal theory from other creator's rights, such as patent and trademark. Although the Statute of Anne was passed in 1709, it had no effect on the Stationers' system until it was used to challenge the Stationers' monopoly in 1767 before the English House of Lords. In a famous case, *Millar v. Taylor* 98 Eng. Rep. 201 (K.B. 1769), a bookseller that was not a member of the Stationers' Company was trying to publish a book after the term of exclusive rights had expired under the Statute of Anne. The Stationers' won the case on the argument that an artist enjoys rights under natural law that do not expire, such as the right to protect the integrity of his work, and that the Stationers' Company was the guardian of the author's natural rights.

Seven years later the Stationers' Company faced another challenge to its monopoly in *Donaldson v. Beckett* 1 Eng Rep. 837 (H.L. 1774). This time the result was different, and this case is the reason that the Statute of Anne is the foundation of American copyright law. Again, an independent bookseller was seeking the right to publish a book for which the rights under the Statute of Anne had expired. This time the House of Lords panel, consisting of eleven judges, recognized that the author did indeed have natural rights in a created work, but that once the book had been published, only the rights to reproduce and exploit the work were entitled to legal protection; the protection provided by the Statute of Anne.

At the time, English authors were happy with the result of *Donaldson v. Beckett* because it once and for all smashed the oppressive system of monopoly and censorship of publishing held by the Stationers' Company. In addition, as booksellers were concerned only with the profits to be realized from publishing, they readily recognized an author's creative rights over the work itself, as is the custom in the industry then and now. The *Donaldson* decision was reflective of attitudes all over Europe to take the control of artistic endeavors out of the hands of royalty. The intention was to place legal authority in the legislature, and this intention was attractive to the anti-royal Americans.

During this time, the theory of natural law continued to be discussed, written about, and explained by scholars, thinkers, and revolutionaries. It was the primary basis for the writings of Thomas Jefferson in our own Declaration of Independence in 1775.[14]

> We hold these Truths to be self evident, that all Men are created equal, that they are endowed by their Creator with certain inalienable Rights, that among these are Life, Liberty and the Pursuit of Happiness...

The phrase "inalienable rights" refers to natural rights. When the Declaration of Independence was published, it incited the French to declare their independence as well, based upon the same rights, which they termed the "Rights of Man." Among the Rights of Man recognized were the natural rights of artists. In the years following the French Revolution, this new concept of artists rights as natural rights spread to other European countries, who were also declaring their independence—such as Belgium, the Netherlands, Italy, and Germany.[15]

History has shown that when a society has determined to recognize the rights of the individual in declaring their freedom from oppression or control, it has been based on the principles of natural law. In addition, the flourishing of art and culture, along with legal protection for artistic rights, has paralleled the adoption in a society of the principals of natural law. It may be said that the more evolved or enlightened a people, the greater their official recognition of natural law rights.

3

The Formation of the Berne Union

Early Efforts to Protect International Copyright

Although other forms of art were being created during this period throughout Europe and the newly-formed American colonies, the establishment of laws and legal precedent over the treatment of a creator's rights arose out of disputes involving the field of publishing. It is also from the field of publishing—that is, book authors—that a new way of protecting artistic rights arose.

With the development of the printing press, written works were easily reproduced and exploited, even across international lines. For authors, this presented a problem. The copyright laws of each country only protected works from being copied without the author's permission within that country. It therefore became an economical practice for publishers to sell books written by foreign authors and save having to pay any royalties to the author.

The protests of authors and publishers who were facing unfair competition from their own books resulted in several treaties between countries, promising not to pirate the other country's books. The treaties, however, were usually bilateral, meaning between two countries, and policing the copyrights was getting tedious for everyone concerned.

In 1858 the first Congress on Literary and Artistic Property was convened in Brussels.[16] It was attended by over 300 people, including representatives of each major European country. Even the United

States of America sent a delegate. The participants discussed the dilemma of protecting artistic works across international lines and several broad areas of agreement were reached. They formed a committee to draft a resolution that could be adopted by all countries. Successive meetings in 1861 and 1877 resulted in more resolutions, but the project for a draft universal law quietly lapsed.[17]

The Berne Treaty

Finally the artists took matters into their own hands. In 1878, the *Société des gens de letters* organized an international literary congress in Paris with representatives from three continents. Victor Hugo presided over the event, which passed a number of resolutions acknowledging the natural and perpetual rights of artists.[18] The congress established the International Literary Association which, when expanded to include artists in all media, became *l'Association littéraire et artistique internationale.* The first president of the Association was Victor Hugo. They organized three additional conferences—in 1882, 1883 and 1884—before convening the 1886 Berne Convention, where a global copyright treaty was finally signed.

The Berne Convention for the Protection of Literary and Artistic Works was signed in Berne, Switzerland by 10 countries: United Kingdom, Haiti, Italy, Switzerland, Tunisia, Liberia, Germany, Spain, France and Belgium. The treaty was revised at five later conventions: Berlin (1908), Rome (1928), Brussels (1948), Stockholm (1967) and Paris (1971). At the 1928 Rome convention, the treaty was expanded to include moral rights protection and broadened to encompass every production in the literary, scientific, and artistic realms. After the Brussels convention, in which cinematographic and photographic works were added, the membership in Berne doubled. The protection of artistic rights offered by the Berne Treaty is so complete that intellectual property experts the world over recognize it as the "standard *par excellence* of copyright protection."[19]

The Berne Treaty brought the theory and focus of artistic rights back to the basics of natural law. The theory sees the foundation of the rights of an author as part of the very nature of things. Laws concerning intellectual property have no other purpose but to recognize the existence of the author's rights, and to give them a more precise formulation. Such rights are not created by the laws, because they have always existed in the conscience of humankind. Copyright is thus viewed as a natural right growing out of natural law.[20]

Artists' Rights As Human Rights

It is remarkable that the Berne Treaty could so strongly rely on natural law considering that, beginning in the 19th century, the concept of natural law in governmental policy had given way to the "social contract."[21] It was generally believed that the good of society as a whole took precedence over the rights of the individual. Natural law, then, was nearly forgotten altogether until World War II, when the idea of rights which exist independent of governmental laws resurfaced. The world was shocked to learn of the atrocities committed by the Nazi government in Germany. The actions the Nazis had taken to imprison, rob, torture, or kill anyone they deemed deserving were completely consistent with the laws they had enacted. Thus their actions were not, per se, illegal, and they argued that their actions were for the good of their society. It therefore became clear that law and morality could not be based on a political ideology. Human thought gelled to the consensus that certain actions are wrong, no matter what, and that all people have certain basic rights.[22]

The recognition of inalienable rights was resurrected from the ashes of World War II, but not as natural law. The world coined a new term for the concept, "human rights." In 1948 the United Nations Universal Declaration of Human Rights was finalized and endorsed by each member of the United Nations. Although they are not actually laws in force in every country, they are seen as guidelines that each country in the global community should endeavor to follow in order for people to be able to live contently. However, there is a European Court of Human Rights that hears cases of human rights violations and renders judgments enforceable within the European community.

The international development of laws regarding the rights of creators have become increasingly based on the natural law theory. For example, the moral rights of authors are specifically recognized in the United Nations Universal Declaration of Human Rights:

> Everyone has the right to the protection of the moral and material interests resulting from any scientific, literary or artistic production of which he is the author.[23]

PART II
The Ideal and The Reality

Moral Rights

In addition to the international protection from unauthorized reproduction and distribution of artistic works that the original drafters sought, the Berne Treaty provides protection for the other natural rights of artists. This recognition of the unique nature of intellectual property is how The Berne Convention for the Protection of Literary and Artistic Works became known as the standard *par excellence* of copyright protection. Article 6*bis* of the treaty very specifically protects art and artists with the following language:

> (1) Independently of the author's economic rights, and even after the transfer of the said rights, the author shall have the right to claim authorship of the work and to object to any distortion, mutilation or other modification of, or other derogatory action in relation to, the said work, which would be prejudicial to his honor or reputation.

> (2) The rights granted to the author in accordance with the preceding paragraph shall, after his death, be maintained, at least until the expiry of the economic rights, and shall be exercisable by the persons or institutions authorized by the legislation of the country where protection is claimed. However, those countries whose legislation, at the moment of ratification of or accession to this Act, does not provide for the protection after the death of the author of all the rights set out in the preceding paragraph may provide that some of these rights may, after his death, cease to be maintained.

> (3) The means of redress for safeguarding the rights granted by this Article shall be governed by the legislation of the country where protection is claimed.[24]

The rights set forth in this section are commonly referred to as "moral rights," sometimes referred to as *droit moral*. Throughout the centuries moral rights, as they have been articulated, can be divided into four broad categories:

- The right to receive name credit (including pseudonym or anonymous if preferred) for having created a work.

- The right to decide when a work is completed or ready to be exhibited, displayed or otherwise made available to the public.

- The right to protection of a work after it has been sold from alteration, modification, or destruction without the artist's prior consent.

- The right to receive a resale royalty on future sales of a work if the price goes up.

4

The Right of Paternity—
The Right to Name Credit

The moral right of paternity is an ancient natural right, recognized as inextricably linked to the act of creation. Without a doubt, the right of paternity is also closely related to the commercial interests of an artist.

Sometimes an artist will take name credit as the only payment for a work or service in order to become known. The name credits can then be traded upon to receive more, paying, work in the future. In addition, name credit provides the reward of name recognition—a valuable commodity for artists when it comes to marketing their works.

The right of paternity is such a sensible companion to creating that it, along with its companion moral rights, is the law in 150 countries around the world, including—believe it or not—the People's Republic of China. Moreover, in France, the birthplace of modern moral rights laws, the law specifically states that an artist cannot sign away these rights in a contract. This is completely consistent with the inalienable nature of moral rights.

After all, once an artist has signed a contract he or she is no less the creator of an artwork. Moral rights, as human rights, are natural rights that accompany our existence as human beings. A contract that waives the human right not to be held in prison for no reason is not valid, and similarly, any other contract designed to circumvent a person's human rights is, in reality, invalid.

Artist As Slave

In a very oppressive contract, an art dealer completely held a painter named Guille under his thumb. In exchange for a regular monthly salary the artist was to deliver to the art dealer at least twenty paintings per month for a period of ten years. Under the contract, the artist was to sign some of the paintings with a pseudonym chosen by the art dealer and leave other paintings with no name at all. On top of that, the art dealer would select fifteen of the twenty paintings delivered by the artist each month, after which the artist was required to destroy the remaining five paintings. Not surprisingly, the artist reached a point where he snapped and refused to continue. The art dealer went to court to enforce the contract and, much to his surprise, the court released the artist from the contract entirely because the terms were oppressively harsh and because the contract violated the artist's basic right to receive credit under his own name for his work.[25]

Although the right to receive name credit is relatively easy to protect, its companion is the right not to receive name credit. The reasons for this are not always so obvious, because on first instinct, it would seem that anyone would want to receive credit for what they had created. Sometimes, though, for personal reasons, a creator may not want his name on his work.

Fal-De-Ra and Fiddle-Dee-Dee

A medical doctor wrote a poem, a rhyming story, about Christmas for the amusement of his children. At that time, Christmas was not even recognized as a holiday, much less celebrated as it is today. The man, a respected physician, did not want anyone to know that he engaged in so frivolous an endeavor as to write a poem about Christmas. However, his children liked it so much that they shared it with their friends, and copies of it began to circulate. It was first published anonymously in the *Sentinel*, a Troy, New York newspaper on December 23, 1823. The little story was so popular that Dr.

Clement Clark Moore finally agreed to take credit for his work, "The Night Before Christmas."[26]

Today we think of "The Night Before Christmas" as a depiction of the way Christmas is traditionally celebrated in this country. Actually, the poem played a large role, historically, in bringing about the current secular celebration of the holidays.

Sometimes an artist's desire to not receive name credit derives from more than mere bashfulness. Once a work has been altered, for example, it is no longer what the artist created. Removing the artist's name from a work will prevent someone who does not know the artist's work from seeing the altered version and forming an erroneous perception of the artist's style or talent.

While an altered work may affect the artist's reputation, the right to receive or withhold name credit also has an effect on the salability of the artwork itself. Naturally, fame can be a factor. When the Nobel Prize winning author Gabriel García Márquez was a young journalist, he helped a young sailor who had survived a shipwreck to write about his experience. The account was first published in a South American newspaper with the sailor's name as the author. In 1989, *The Story of a Shipwrecked Sailor* was published in book form under the name Gabriel García Márquez and the author, in his foreword, had this to say:

> I have not reread this story in fifteen years. It seems worthy of publication, but I have never quite understood the usefulness of publishing it. I find it depressing that the publishers are not so much interested in the merit of the story as in the name of the author, which, much to my sorrow, is also that of a fashionable writer. If it is now published in the form of a book, that is because I agreed without thinking about it very much, and I am not a man to go back on his word.

Sometimes, however, the artist does not want to have his name become famous as a national joke.

And You Can Take That To The Bank

In 1910 a famous French artist named Merson, who had designed the French 100 franc note, wrote a letter to the Bank of France telling them that he was upset by the changes the bank had made to his design when printing the currency. The changes had distorted his original design and resulted in public criticism of the bank note. In 1914 the artist wrote another letter in an effort to repair his reputation and the letter was published in a Paris newspaper. Some years later, the same distortion was shown on the 50 franc note which Merson also designed. The ridicule the artist suffered on the lips of his compatriots, who hated the money, was the bane of his existence. By 1936 the artist had died and the heirs of his estate went to court, forcing the bank, over its objection, to remove the artist's signature from any future printing of the money.[27]

It can also happen that the artist's name becomes more important than the artwork itself when the artist is famous. Stephen King experienced this phenomenon. For years he had been such a prolific producer of fiction that his publisher became concerned that he would glut the market and reduce the salability of his books. They insisted that he limit himself to one novel per year. King agreed, but secretly kept on writing under the pseudonym Richard Bachman, selling his output to another publishing house. Richard Bachman's fourth and highest selling novel was *Thinner*, which sold 28,000 copies with no marketing. At that point, Bachman's true identity was discovered on a copyright form. Sales of the book *Thinner* by Stephen King soared to 280,000.[28] Of course, it's important to protect a name with that kind of selling power.

There is no reason why artists should not be able to put their name on their works if they want to, or to have their name taken off something that is not their work. The market value of a work of art will not suffer in the least if the creator's name is on it, and it may even be helped. On the other hand, the market value may be reduced if the creator's name is removed. But if an artist did not create the work which is being sold, then that artist's name does not belong on it.

5

The Right of Integrity—
The Right to Protect A Work
From Alteration

Safeguarding the integrity of the artistic expression is the paramount goal of moral rights. The right of integrity is associated almost exclusively with the personal expression of the artist. If the work is changed, the message embodied in the work is changed. This also affects the artist's livelihood, becoming another aspect of the commercial interests of the artist. After all, the artist's reputation depends on the accurate depiction of his or her work in public.

With advances in technology, created works can be reproduced or altered easily and inexpensively. Thus it has become easy to forget, or take for granted, the effort that went into the original concept—the original expression. As Gertrude Stein said of Picasso in *The Autobiography of Alice B. Toklas*:

> Sure, she said, as Pablo once remarked, when you make a thing, it is so complicated making it that it is bound to be ugly, but those that do it after you they don't have to worry about making it and they can make it pretty, and so everybody can like it when the others make it.

Imagine how radical Picasso's work looked when it first came out. He had taken the rules of perspective and shadow and shattered them with a brush. Although many artists used Picasso's technique to achieve a level of commercial success in their day, it is Picasso, the inventor, whose works draw the highest prices at auction now.

There are two aspects to the right of integrity. The first aspect concerns staying true to the original spirit of the work when showing it in a different form or different medium (making a movie from a book, publishing a painting or a photograph in a book, etc.). The second aspect relates to altering the work itself.

In either case, this right involves the exhibition of a created work to the public. Controlling what the public sees also controls the public's perception of the work. People will respond to what they see. They need to see the actual work to be able to form any kind of opinion about it or reaction to it. You might guess that perception can be affected by hanging a painting upside down or by displaying a work that is intended to remain indoors outside, where the elements can affect it. There are countless ways in which an artwork can be changed, even in the exhibition of it, which will affect how it is perceived.

De Chirico

In 1950 the Italian artist Giorgio De Chirico was honored with the decision to be featured at the one-man show exhibition sponsored twice each year by the Venice Biennale, an event of national prominence. Works by the artist were gathered from private and public collections for a retrospective exhibition. Rather than being flattered, the artist was upset. He felt that the show misrepresented the entirety of his body of work by including more of his earlier works and fewer of his later works.

It was generally thought by critics and art experts that De Chirico's earlier works were really his best works. The artist, however, felt that he had significantly advanced his abilities through his later works and that it was the later works, not the earlier works, which constituted his best art. The artist sued the exhibit organizers and the Italian court agreed that a one-man show at the Biennale was important enough to protect the artist's right to be accurately and fairly represented in it.

Although an Italian Court of Appeal overturned the ruling five years later, the issue was no longer relevant to the event.[29]

When a work is adapted to another medium, it is generally recognized that some changes will have to be done in the process. It is virtually impossible to transfer a work to another medium and have it remain exactly the same. However, the people creating the adaptation should endeavor to be true to the *spirit* of the original work by preserving its message.

Millet's Angelus

In 1911, two publishers were fighting in court over which had the right to publish a reproduction of "The Angelus," a famous painting by Jean-François Millet. The artist's son, Charles Millet joined the lawsuit, claiming neither publisher should have the right to print copies of the painting because each of them had representations which distorted and falsified the original work of art. Upon comparison, the court acknowledged that the reproductions brightened the lighting of the original painting, made objects look vulgar, added a bonnet to a person's head and a scarf around the woman's neck, and changed an evening scene to one suffused by a glaring noonday sun. The court concluded that no one who looked at the reproductions would have believed Millet was a great artist. In the interest of protecting the "superior interests of the human genius," the court stopped the publishers, "individuals with dubious intentions guided by some transient fashion or profit motives."[30]

This example provides the crucial understanding of what is meant by the perpetual rights of the artist. When those publishers wanted to use Millet's art, he had long been deceased and the time limit which the law places on exclusive commercial rights (copyright) had expired. The painting was available for copying, as it was hanging in the Louvre museum in Paris and no one owned the copying rights.

When the copyright on a work expires, the work goes into what's called the "public domain," meaning that anyone can make copies of the art and sell the copies without having to pay for that right. For example, when the copyright of the film "It's A Wonderful Life" expired, the film went into the public domain. Every television channel began showing the film at all hours because they didn't have to pay anyone for the right to exhibit it. It was later determined that the rights in the soundtrack had not expired and the wonderful free-for-all stopped.

Since Millet's heir did not own the marketing rights anymore, he could not stop anyone from making copies of his father's works and using them for advertising, or selling them outright. However, he still had the rights to protect the integrity of the work, and if he had not exercised that right he could easily have seen other mutilations of his father's art, until people no longer knew or remembered what the original art expressed.

The artist's ability to communicate through his or her art becomes clouded by an inaccurate representation of the work and the artist's future market value could be negatively changed.

Monty Python v. ABC

In the 1970's the American Broadcasting Company (ABC) bought the rights to show the British comedy series, "Monty Python's Flying Circus," on American television. To allow for commercial interruptions, which British television did not have, ABC cut some portions of the skits and changed their order according to length. When the creators of "Monty Python's Flying Circus" saw a tape of the American broadcast, they were horrified.

The shows had been designed with running jokes and comic timing which were lost when the skits were moved around. In the case of one skit, ABC simply cut off the end of it, *including the punch line*, because it contained the word "fart", and ABC claimed the Federal Communications Commission would have made them take it out anyway. Consequently, the entire skit did not make sense and was not funny. The Monty Python creators sued ABC in an American court and won damages for the violation of the integrity of their work.[31]

After the Monty Python episodes were first aired on ABC, the American media coined the term "British humor" for comedy originating in England that was not perceived as funny in this country. British comedy has never quite fully recovered from the label. The Monty Python case is an example of how the right of integrity is intended to prevent mutilation, alteration, modification, destruction or any other "tion" from occurring to a created work—except, of course, appreciation.

It bears noting that it was not the original owner of the work, the BBC, that caused the alterations to the Monty Python shows. With television and film, violations of moral rights do not usually come from the original producers. Even the original producer takes the completed work and markets it *as it is* because the producer is also one of the creators.

It is when ownership of the created work is changed that the new owners take it upon themselves to cut up or alter the work, taking the parts they like the best and trying to find new ways to market the original work. There is no such thing as a "new and improved" work of art. This was proven with the process known as colorization, in which whole themes of films were altered by imposing arbitrary color tones onto black and white films.

Similarly, it has become virtually impossible to watch a feature film on commercial television, when advertisements can take up as much as 25 minutes of each hour of the broadcast. When four minutes of a film, even that edited from the original, are sandwiched between two five minute commercial interruptions, the viewer is not receiving what was communicated by the original creative expression. A mystery thriller loses its suspense when the audience is asked to buy a car just when the clues are starting to fit together.

Technology Advances and Movies Talk

In 1929, an actor who played the role of Father Martin in a silent film called "The Miraculous Life of Saint Teresa" sued the producer when sound was added and the voice of another actor was dubbed in for Father Martin. The actor who played the part said that the voice of the other actor violated the integrity of his performance. He stated that he suffered injury to his reputation and his ability to get future acting roles. The court agreed.[32]

As far as films go, actors do not usually own any marketing rights to the film. That is, they are not usually the copyright owners. They usually are paid for their performance only. If they are famous enough for their name to be used to help market the film, then they might be entitled to receive some of the revenues generated by exhibiting the film. However, this payment is only in exchange for the actor's performance, and it is completely separate from the marketing rights, which belong to the copyright owner. Once the actor's performance has been incorporated into the film the marketing value of that performance, that work of art, belongs to whoever owns the copyright of the film.

Yet as a creative expression, the actor's performance has artistic value and it is directly related to the artist's reputation and ability to get future work.

The Patriotism of Shostakovich

Right after World War II, 20th Century Fox released a film about Russian international spy activity called "The Iron Curtain." The producers used the music of four Russian composers, including Shostakovich, for the soundtrack. The film was not very flattering in the way it portrayed Russian foreign policy. At the time, Russia was considered a threat to the U.S. All four composers sued 20th Century Fox Film Corp. to prevent the showing of the film for the reasons that it was politically objectionable and made the composers seem like they were not loyal to their homeland, which was in violation of their artistic rights. In France the composers won, but in the United States, they lost.[33]

Just like Millet's heir, Shostakovich did not own the marketing rights to his music anymore. The copyright had expired. Yet as the creator of the music, he still had a very real interest in protecting his work. He felt that the portrayal, or exhibition, of his music in that film was done in such a way as to alter the expression of it.

Also like Millet's heir, Shostakovich's actions were taken to prevent the alteration of his expression in other instances and the eventual obscurity of the original feeling of the music he composed. The composer did not want his music to be perpetually tied to those film images in the same way people later linked the fourth movement of Beethoven's Ninth Symphony ("Ode to Joy") with the horrendous torture scenes in the film, "A Clockwork Orange."

The events described in the following two examples do not violate copyright, although it is very clear that *something* was violated.

Sculpture by Numbers

A sculptor named DuPassage created a marble statue consisting of three separate groups of figures which were all part of the same piece. He sold the statue and agreed that the purchaser could make copies of the statue and sell them. The sculptor later learned that the purchaser had cut up the statue and was selling copies of each of the three parts of the composition as separate works of art by the artist. DuPassage brought a lawsuit against the purchaser in France and won. The court recognized that by cutting up the statue the purchaser had "disrupted the unity of an artistic creation and adulterated its character." Perhaps certain obscenity laws might also have applied.[34]

Waste Not, Want Not

In 1936, a sculptor named Sudre was honored by his native village with a request to create a piece for a public fountain. The artist created a statue of a woman wearing the local costume. Over time the elements took their toll on the statue, and the city council decided to remove it and break it up. Later, when the artist visited the village again, he found pieces of his statue being used to fill holes in the road. He sued his home town and was awarded substantial damages for the violation of the integrity of his art.[35]

This last example is like watching a spectacular slip and fall on ice. Our first instinct is to laugh, even though the person going through the experience is suffering. Surely there were other, less degrading, ways to remove a statue that had deteriorated in the weather and could not be restored. Presumably the artist's trips home were few and far between, since he did not know about the decline and removal of the statue and only noticed pieces of it in the road some years later. It may have been that the townspeople also felt slighted by an artist they had tried to honor. When it comes to creative endeavors, there are a lot of emotions involved which do not apply to any other type of business transaction and people take a disregard of their artistic rights, or their appreciation, personally.

Moral rights, being part of the natural law doctrine, will not be allowed to interfere with the natural rights of others.

Al Fresco

In 1934 a French painter named Lacasse was commissioned to paint a fresco in the church of a small French town. However, the bishop—who was considered the actual owner of the church—was out of town and didn't know about it. After the frescoes were finished, word reached the bishop that the frescoes were done and there had been some controversy. The bishop went to look at the artwork and decided that it was inappropriate for the church. He ordered the frescoes to be painted over. The insulted artist tried to stop the action, but the court decided that the owner of the property, who did not commission, nor even know about the artwork, had the right to get rid of it without being liable for any damages.[36]

Tired of Blushing

In 1912, in Germany, a homeowner commissioned an artist to paint a mural on the side of his house. Later, the residents became offended by the nudity portrayed in the mural and the owner hired another artist to paint clothes on the figures. The original artist claimed the house owner had violated his artistic rights. A German court agreed this was true, but added that the artist's rights would not have been violated if the homeowner had completely painted over the entire mural.[37]

When dealing with a work of art which is about as immovable as art gets—a mural—the value of the art cannot be maintained without considering the value of the thing the art is on. A mural is created at the outset with elements of permanence and impermanence. Usually it is outside, so most artists coat the final image with something that will protect the expression from both the natural elements and graffiti. In this sense, it is created to last.

However, it will always be subject to the control of the owner of the thing on which the artwork is applied. Just as an owner can commission the mural to be applied, so the same owner, or another owner, can have the mural removed. As in the last example, an alteration of the artistic expression is a violation of the integrity of the art. The alteration will change the expression. Elimination of the artwork altogether, however, will not change what the original artwork said. It will simply silence it. That is why murals are, by their nature, very loud. They have an uncertain time period in which they may speak, so for whatever time they have they shout at the top of their lungs to anyone who comes near.

Aside from the obvious visible changes to a work of artistic expression, altering it affects its commercial value. It clouds the perception of the artist's ability, thus having a direct effect on the artist's reputation and income. Mutilation of artwork is not just bad for the art. It also hurts the artist, any person who has bought, or who has the exclusive right to sell the art, and the public as a whole.

6

The Right of Exhibition—
The Right to Decide When A
Work Is Finished

It makes perfect sense that the artist who is creating something is the only person who knows when the artwork is finished. Generally a work is not finished until the artist says it is, or relinquishes possession of it, whichever comes first.

The possession distinction is important, because many artists—especially writers—never feel that their work is "finished." Every time they look at it they see something they want to change and completion means perfection: a persistent, but elusive temptress. In this circumstance, the best an artist can do is to pass the artwork on to the mode of exhibition and court perfection in the next work.

Even throwing a work in the trash does not mean that the artist considers it to be "finished." An example of this was illustrated by the painter Charles Camoin in Paris in 1925. The artist was unhappy with some of his paintings, so he slashed them to pieces and threw them out. Someone found the ruined paintings, restored them, and put them up for sale at an art auction. Camoin was able to legally prevent the trash picker from selling the restored paintings. The Parisian court declared that if the artist did not want his paintings exhibited that was entirely his prerogative, so the finder owned the cut-up pieces he found and nothing more.[38]

Once again, the right of exhibition is connected to the livelihood of the artist. If the work is not finished, it cannot possibly represent the artist's style.

Best of Both Worlds for Painter Rouault

In a deal most artists only dream about, a painter named Rouault was under exclusive contract with a famous art dealer of his time to deliver all of his artistic output for a fee. This amounted to some 806 paintings which were kept in a locked studio provided by the art dealer. The artist had a key to the studio and entered at his convenience to apply finishing touches to his paintings. During this arrangement, the art dealer died. The art dealer's heirs claimed they owned the paintings in the studio. The artist said he wasn't finished with them. Before the paintings were finished, according to the artist, they still belonged to him.[39]

If this business relationship had involved any other type of property besides art, the heirs would likely have won possession of the items, but they weren't; that is because no one besides Rouault could have finished his paintings. Looking at the arrangement between the artist and the art dealer, each party came to the agreement with something. Each side contributed to the total value of the artwork. The artist produced the paintings, and the art dealer—who was a skilled salesman known for his abilities—created the demand for the artwork. For this, the art dealer provided a studio to the artist and paid the artist a set fee. The dealer allowed the artist to finish the paintings to his satisfaction, thereby enhancing the quality of the artwork, which in turn increased the sales price. The entire sales price was pocketed by the dealer.

Each party relied upon the talent of the other to form a successful business enterprise. By maintaining the paintings in a studio he provided, the art dealer established himself as the only art dealer selling Roualt's art. As the artist's work became more well-known, the demand for it grew, and so did the sales price. The increase in demand and price gave value to the exclusivity aspect of the relationship. The exclusivity was another element that the artist contributed to the arrangement in addition to his paintings. The moment when the paintings were finished signaled the end of the artist's half of the arrangement and the beginning of the art dealer's half. Clearly the unfinished paintings were still the artist's.

There is still another way to look at the concept of "finished."

Taking His Records and Going Home

A composer named Léo Ferré wrote the musical soundtrack for a film. In the course of the final editing of the film, portions of the composer's music were also cut. The artist objected and claimed that he did not agree that the film was "finished" in the way that it portrayed his musical contribution. The composer was permitted to withdraw his music from the film altogether.[40]

It is the finished product which contains the artistic expression, even though someone may look at a work that is almost finished and feel that they understand what it is all about. Often the artist saves the best for last, and a work only *seems* to be finished until it actually is. Sometimes the final touch, or the final track, or the final edit is the last little turn of the focus wheel that makes the impact of the artwork razor sharp.

7

The Right to a Resale Royalty

An artist who has created an incredible work of art has a moral right to be able to share in its ongoing commercial success. The beholder's response to the artwork is an indication of the artist's talent. The reputation for the talent gives the artist fame. Fame increases the sales price, or market value, of the artwork. The obvious purpose of the resale royalty is to minimize the possibility of an artist dying famous, but penniless, while around the corner, a dealer in his works is making fabulous profits selling them.[41] It is the one area in which moral rights and economic rights overlap completely.

The concept of a resale royalty applies to maintain the recognition of the artist for the work. It also addresses the inequity of the cash-poor artist who may have sold his or her work for less than its reasonable market value just to be able to get some money to live on. Artists, before they become famous, often have no idea how much money they should ask for their work. Someone more familiar with the marketplace would know, but the artist doesn't always know someone like that. Sometimes, then, artists sell their works for what they think they can get and it turns out the works are worth a lot more than that in the marketplace. The resale royalty is a way of balancing out the artist's lack of market knowledge against their obvious artistic ability.

8

Artists' Rights, American Style

Fledgling Copyright Law in the U.S.

Although the United States of America was founded upon the principals of natural law, its recognition of inalienable rights did not inspire the same bold assertions on behalf of artists that European countries declared. Instead, American law characterizes the artist's work as more of an object of commerce than as a product of the spirit.[42] The U.S. Constitution provides simply that Congress shall have the power:

> To promote the Progress of Science and useful Arts, by securing for limited Times to Authors and Inventors the exclusive Right to their respective Writings and Discoveries

Da Silva provides a good characterization of how American laws regarding created works are not based on natural law, but on the outdated concept of the social contract as evidenced by the constitutional language. While other, older countries create their laws to clarify and codify rights that are already deemed to exist in the person of the artist, the United States takes the view that the enacted law is what creates the rights and the purpose of the law is to achieve a socially desirable end. Thus the rights of the individual must compete with the "greater good." In practice, we find the good of the many being spoken for by a few private interests.

In 1790, the young American government passed its first law of copyright, based on the English Statute of Anne. Presumably, the intent of the Statute of Anne—to remove publishing from the hands of the sovereign—appealed to our early legislators, who wanted nothing to do with anything royal.

It is clear, though, from the first copyright case decided by the United States Supreme Court, *Wheaton v. Peters*, in 1834, that the concept of artists rights was not thoroughly defined in this country. The case was decided in line with the English case of *Donaldson v. Beckett*, holding that the author's rights are derived from the copyright statute and are limited to what is stated in the statute. The *Donaldson* decision made sense in England, as it freed authors from the monopoly of a system implemented by the sovereign. Without such a history in this country, however, the ruling was based on a complete lack of understanding of artistic right and confusion.[43]

The U.S. in International Copyright Relations

The European efforts to institute an international copyright treaty provided an opportunity for the United States, who was present at each meeting, to be educated as to the nature of artists' rights. The United States was also represented at each Berne Convention meeting, always sending a representative who did not have authority to sign the treaty, but who always strongly recommended that the U.S. join. In 1886, at the first signing of the Berne Treaty, the U.S. representative was perfectly honest about the reasons the U.S. was not signing the treaty. He issued a general declaration stating that, while the U.S. agreed in principal with the idea of international copyright protection, it saw immense obstacles to achieving it, particularly the threat posed to American manufacturing interests involved in the production of copyright works.[44]

As it turned out, the United States was the most prolific copyright pirate in the world. It not only refused to enact any laws to protect foreign authors, but it actually appeared to encourage piracy.[45] It seems that for one hundred years after the enactment of the first copyright statute in this country, American publishers were printing and selling copies of books by foreign authors, particularly British authors, without paying any royalties to them. Naturally, American authors felt cheated, and foreign authors felt robbed by the unfair competition between American books and cheap British reprints that were offered to the public at sometimes one quarter the price of books by domestic authors.

Among the foreign authors most incensed by this practice was Charles Dickens, who wrote to his biographer of his efforts to bring about some change in the system in 1842:

> I spoke, as you know, of international copyright, at Boston; and I spoke of it again at Hartford. My friends were paralyzed with wonder at such audacious daring. The notion that I, a man alone by himself, in America, should venture to suggest to the Americans that there was one point on which they were neither just to their own countrymen nor to us, actually struck the boldest dumb! Washington Irving, Prescott, Hoffman, Bryant, Halleck, Dana, Washington Allston—every man who writes in this country is devoted to the question, and not one of them dares to raise his voice and complain of the atrocious state of the law. It is nothing that of all men living, I am the greatest loser by it. It is nothing that I have a claim to speak and be heard. The wonder is that a breathing man can be found with temerity enough to suggest to the Americans the possibility of their having done wrong. I wish you could have seen the faces that I saw, down both sides of the table at Hartford, when I began to talk about Scott. I wish you could have heard how I gave it out. My blood so boiled as I thought of the monstrous injustice that I felt as if I were twelve feet high when I thrust it down their throats.[46]

The same thing was happening to American authors in Britain. Sandison points out that Longfellow, for example, complained that although he had twenty-two publishers in England and Scotland, "only four of them took the slightest notice of my existence, even so far as to send me a copy of the book."[47] It bears mentioning that Dickens managed to get publishing contracts with two large U.S. publishers so he could get paid for his work.

In 1879, a number of prominent American writers, including Long-fellow, Oliver Wendell Holmes and Ralph Waldo Emerson tried to replicate the activities of *l'Association littéraire et artistique internationale* and signed a resolution in favor of an international copyright, but publishers would have none of it.

The foreign piracy of American works finally began to take its toll on the business interests of U.S. publishing houses, and authors began to find allies in the fight for international copyright protection. Even President Grover Cleveland, in an annual message to Congress at the end of 1886, referred to the United States' entry into the Berne Treaty.[48] Although a growing group of authors and large publishers, including Little, Brown & Co., advocated American membership in the Berne Convention, the U.S. would not join the treaty for another 103 years.

Although one hurdle had been overcome, a new and stronger obstacle to the international protection of artistic rights took its place. As Ringer observed, the development of radio and motion picture technology during the 1920's—soon to be joined by the medium of television—introduced new interests into the orbit of intellectual properties and made more difficult the task of securing agreement on proposals to effect a general revision of the copyright law.[49] It wasn't personal; it was business.

The rights of artists, though, are personal. In particular, the moral rights of artists have variously been referred to as the "rights of personality" in the outward representation of one's innermost self. A created work carries the artist's ideas, conceptions, opinions or thoughts, under his or her own name, to the public. Intellectual property is an intangible made accessible to society by being attached to the tangible.[50]

U.S. Joins the Berne Union

Despite the creeping progress of artists' rights protection in this country, we finally joined the Berne Treaty in 1989. Ironically, it was the same interests initially opposed to U.S. entry into the Berne Treaty who later requested entry in order to protect *their* property outside the United States. In the 1980's, videocassette rental paved the way to an entirely new source of film revenue. As a result, video piracy grew rampant, especially in other countries. Studios and producers weren't getting any revenue from video sales and rentals, and there was nothing they could do about it because the countries where piracy was discovered honored the Berne Treaty and the United States did not. Finally, policymakers decided it cost too much money to avoid becoming a part of the same copyright treaty as everyone else. In 1989 the United States became a member of the Berne Treaty.

When considering the Berne Treaty for ratification, American lawmakers had to decide how to enforce Article 6bis. The treaty includes an option that Article 6bis does not have to be accepted if the country seeking to join Berne already has laws in place that provide the same protection for art and artists as 6bis. At that time Congress, with the help of a battalion of lawyers sent by the film, television and recording industries, determined that American laws protect all the artistic rights that the Berne Treaty, including 6bis, protects. If our laws protect the inalienable rights of all people, then U.S. law does offer this protection.

However, in order to appease the powerful interests from the entertainment sector who wanted the benefits of the Berne Treaty without the obligations of it, Congress also passed Title 17, United States Code, Section 104(c).

(c) Effect of Berne Convention.—

No right or interest in a work eligible for protection under this title may be claimed by virtue of, or in reliance upon, the provisions of the Berne Convention, or the adherence of the United States thereto. Any rights in a work eligible for protection under this title that derive from this title, other Federal or State statutes, or the common law, shall not be expanded or reduced by virtue of, or in reliance upon, the provisions of the Berne Convention, or the adherence of the United States thereto.

That provision is to prevent anyone in the United States from invoking the Berne Treaty to protect their creative rights. The statute is, of course, unconstitutional. Article VI of the United States Constitution states that an international treaty is to be considered the "supreme Law of the Land," taking priority over *all* domestic laws. The Constitution is a higher authority than a federal statute, thus a federal statute that claims that an international treaty is subordinate to the domestic law is contradictory to the Constitution, or unconstitutional.

It is likely that Congress was aware of the Constitutional mandate because, prior to ratifying the treaty, Congress had to revise U.S. copyright law to make it conform to the requirements of the Berne Treaty as a condition of membership. For example, artists are no longer required to use the symbol "©" followed by the year and their names to protect their copyrights.

The question of whether the Berne Treaty can be invoked to protect artistic rights directly has not yet been tested in an American court of law. Based on the language of the U.S. Constitution, it can be and all the moral rights enumerated above are entitled to the full protection of our laws.

Moral Rights in the U.S.

Artist's Royalty

One aspect of moral rights has long existed in the laws of several states, including California and New York, to protect the right of the artist to a resale royalty. There are also provisions in most guild, or collective bargaining, agreements in the entertainment industry to provide for ongoing royalties for artists. In California the Artists Resale Royalty Act is part of the California Civil Code, Section 986. The basic royalty is set forth in the first paragraph.

> (a) Whenever a work of fine art is sold and the seller resides in California or the sale takes place in California, the seller or the seller's

agent shall pay to the artist of such work of fine art or to such artist's agent 5 percent of the amount of such sale. The right of the artist to receive an amount equal to 5 percent of the amount of such sale may be waived only by a contract in writing providing for an amount in excess of 5 percent of the amount of such sale. An artist may assign the right to collect the royalty payment provided by this section to another individual or entity. However, the assignment shall not have the effect of creating a waiver prohibited by this subdivision.

A consortium of art galleries brought two court actions in the first years after California's statute was passed trying to have it declared unconstitutional. The law was upheld on both occasions.

Other Moral Rights

Recognizing the limitations of statutory laws regarding intellectual property, the learned men of the judiciary attempted to fill in the gaps. As the court observed in the Monty Python case:

> …the copyright law should be used to recognize the important role of the artist in our society and the need to encourage production and dissemination of artistic works by providing adequate protection for one who submits his work to the public.[51]

Artists' rights came to be included in the pool of rights, which all people have but no legislature has seen fit to enumerate, the common law. A fairly good definition of "common law" was offered by the English court in *Millar v. Taylor* in 1774:

> These are those rights which are founded on the law of reason. Its grounds, maxims and principals are derived from many different fountains…from natural and moral philosophy, from the civil and canon law, from logic, from the use, custom and conversation among men, collected out of the general disposition of nature and of human kind.

Following that early stumble in *Wheaton v. Peters*, American courts, without any legislation to guide them, have both upheld and denied artists their moral rights as illustrated in the following examples.

The Vargas Girls

Alberto Vargas began his career drawing posters of the Zeigfield performers to advertise the Zeigfield Follies. In 1940 he was still a young, relatively unknown artist, when the publisher of *Esquire* magazine approached him about doing some illustrations for the magazine. They made a contract, and Vargas created illustrations of women for use throughout the publication. Drawn in Vargas' inimitable style, the artwork gave a certain overall "look" to the magazine. The illustrations were a big hit, and the painted ladies became popularly known as the "*Esquire* girls."

In his contract with *Esquire*, Vargas gave the publisher the "right" to use his name on the illustrations. It is likely that the artist thought that he was agreeing with the magazine that they would use his name. The magazine did not see it that way and Vargas' name did not appear anywhere. Vargas was understandably very upset that he was not receiving the recognition he felt he deserved. With his contract in hand, the artist took *Esquire* to court to force the magazine to acknowledge him as the creator of the illustrations. The court was called upon to interpret the contract, and it determined that the specific wording of the agreement *permitted*, but did not *require* the magazine to give name credit to the artist. The court ruled in favor of *Esquire*.[52]

Due to the publicity of the lawsuit, Vargas was able to let the public know that he was the artist responsible for those famous drawings, but in a court of law he could not enforce a right which seems so basic and so logical to a creator.

Fit For A King

In 1992 a film producer sought and received permission to use the title of one of King's novels, *The Lawnmower Man*, as the title of a movie. When the film was completed, it was advertised as "Stephen King's Lawnmower Man." As it turned out, the film was not based on the book and it was a completely different story. Stephen King took legal action and had his name removed from the film as not being his story.[53]

"Imagine" Being Able to Do This

The famous artist John Lennon was able to stop the release of one of his albums because he claimed that poor editing and an "unartistic" cover design amounted to a mutilation of his music, which was on the album.[54]

Sizzling Calder

Alexander Calder is generally regarded as the originator of the modern art form known as the "mobile." In 1958, a black and white Calder mobile called "Pittsburg" was donated by its owner—a private collector—to the city of Pittsburg for its new airport. The city accepted the gift and promptly painted the mobile green and gold: the city's colors. In addition, the new owner of the sculpture changed the configuration of the hanging pieces and proudly placed the altered work in a prominent location in its new airport.

Calder was naturally outraged that someone would have the audacity to alter a work which he had created, and which bore his name. The artist tried to force the City of Pittsburg to either restore the mobile to its original form and color, or remove his name as the creator of the work. The City refused, and the artist had no recourse. The outcry from the public was loud and it lasted for many years. The City finally restored the work to its original colors and form in 1978, years after the artist's death.[55]

Presbyterian Reversal

In the early 1940's, a New York artist named Crimi had been commissioned to paint some frescoes at a Presbyterian church in New York. He completed the work and was paid in full. After the Second World War the frescoes didn't hold the same allure anymore, so after a round of criticism they were obliterated. The artist tried to go to court to order the frescoes restored or removed, but the court said that he had no case because there was no such thing as an artist's moral right in America.[56]

Just because a court refuses to "see" moral rights, doesn't mean they don't exist.

9

Copyright Law

Without using the Berne Treaty, creators are like orphaned waifs who wait outside the kitchen door for leftovers from the feast. They must sustain themselves on laws that were made for someone else. It must be remembered that the army of representatives from the entertainment industry do not go to Washington, D.C. just for the special hearings. They are permanently ensconced there. Artists are not organized in that way, and they do not have the means to lodge highly-paid people who represent their interests in our nation's capitol to affect policy in their favor. The laws passed by Congress in the area of intellectual property reflect this reality.

The area of law designated by Congress for artistic works is copyright law. However, the protections provided by copyright law are very specific and very narrow. In fact, copyright law protects neither the artwork nor the creator of the artwork, but the *owner* of the artwork and its rights to make money with it. A good example of how a work of art "looks" through the lens of copyright law is shown by the following example.

"Lonesome Dove"

A television show called "Lonesome Dove," was made from a script, and was shown on television. An album of the soundtrack to the television show was also released. Later, a book *Lonesome Dove* was written and sold. The book was recorded and released as a "book on tape," and there was background music to accompany the voices who read the book on the tape. Along comes the owner of the rights to the soundtrack of the television show music and claims the music rights for the "book on tape" belong to the soundtrack record company. It was decided that the book right was a separate right from the television show rights, including the soundtrack, and so any rights which came from the book rights do not belong to the owners of the television show rights.[57]

In a copyright scenario, the law is concerned merely with the question of who owns the marketing rights to what. All rights are regarded as commercial, rather than personal, and they belong only to those who have paid for those specific rights, assuming the original artist sold them. The specific rights protected by copyright law are listed in Title 17, United States Code, Section 106.

106.—Exclusive rights in copyrighted works

Subject to sections 107 through 121, the owner of copyright under this title has the exclusive rights to do and to authorize any of the following:

(1) to reproduce the copyrighted work in copies or phonorecords;

(2) to prepare derivative works based upon the copyrighted work;

(3) to distribute copies or phonorecords of the copyrighted work to the public by sale or other transfer of ownership, or by rental, lease, or lending;

(4) in the case of literary, musical, dramatic, and choreographic works, pantomimes, and motion pictures and other audiovisual works, to perform the copyrighted work publicly;

(5) in the case of literary, musical, dramatic, and choreographic works, pantomimes, and pictorial, graphic, or sculptural works, including the individual images of a motion picture or other audiovisual work, to display the copyrighted work publicly; and

(6) in the case of sound recordings, to perform the copyrighted work publicly by means of a digital audio transmission.

Copyright law is not concerned with the work itself as set forth in Title 17, United States Code, Section 202.

> 202—Ownership of copyright as distinct from ownership of material object
>
> Ownership of a copyright, or of any of the exclusive rights under a copyright, is distinct from ownership of any material object in which the work is embodied. Transfer of ownership of any material object, including the copy or phonorecord in which the work is first fixed, does not of itself convey any rights in the copyrighted work embodied in the object; nor, in the absence of an agreement, does transfer of ownership of a copyright or of any exclusive rights under a copyright convey property rights in any material object.

For example, a person who buys a painting doesn't get the right to make copies of it, and the person who owns the rights to make copies does not automatically get ownership of the original painting.

When an artist first creates something, he or she automatically owns all the rights listed in the law, unless it has been created under a "work for hire" contract. Work for hire is discussed in Chapter Eleven—Contract Law. Record companies, publishers, production companies and others who engage in selling created works to the public purchase these rights from the artist. The transfer of rights can only be made in a written document signed by the original artist or the artist's legal representative. Most contracts for the buying and selling of these rights try to include all the artist's rights in a single transaction, but they don't always. The transfer of specific rights is called a "license." The transfer of all rights is called a "grant," or a "transfer," or an "assignment" of copyright. Once the artist has transferred or sold any rights in a work to someone else, the artist no longer has any legal control over those rights or how they are used under copyright law for the next 35 years. The rule is that copyright law follows the ownership of copyright only.

Very narrow exceptions to this rule have been added to the Copyright Act since its inception in 1978. One bold example is the Visual Artists Rights Act, Title 17 United States Code, Section 106A, passed by Congress in 1990 over the strenuous objections of the entertainment industry. To appease those objections, the protections of the new law were strictly limited.

106A—Rights of certain authors to attribution and integrity

(a) Rights of Attribution and Integrity.—

Subject to section 107 and independent of the exclusive rights provided in section 106, the author of a work of visual art—

(1) shall have the right—

(A) to claim authorship of that work, and

(B) to prevent the use of his or her name as the author of any work of visual art which he or she did not create;

(2) shall have the right to prevent the use of his or her name as the author of the work of visual art in the event of a distortion, mutilation, or other modification of the work which would be prejudicial to his or her honor or reputation; and

(3) subject to the limitations set forth in section 113(d), shall have the right—

(A) to prevent any intentional distortion, mutilation, or other modification of that work which would be prejudicial to his or her honor or reputation, and any intentional distortion, mutilation, or modification of that work is a violation of that right, and

(B) to prevent any destruction of a work of recognized stature, and any intentional or grossly negligent destruction of that work is a violation of that right.

A work of visual art is defined in Title 17, United States Code, Section 101.

A "work of visual art" is

(1) a painting, drawing, print, or sculpture, existing in a single copy, in a limited edition of 200 copies or fewer that are signed and consecutively numbered by the author, or, in the case of a sculpture, in multiple cast, carved, or fabricated sculptures of 200 or fewer that are consecutively numbered by the author and bear the signature or other identifying mark of the author; or

(2) a still photographic image produced for exhibition purposes only, existing in a single copy that is signed by the author, or in a limited edition of 200 copies or fewer that are signed and consecutively numbered by the author.

A work of visual art does not include

(A)(i) any poster, map, globe, chart, technical drawing, diagram, model, applied art, motion picture or other audiovisual work, book, magazine, newspaper, periodical, data base, electronic information service, electronic publication, or similar publication;

(ii) any merchandising item or advertising, promotional, descriptive, covering, or packaging material or container;

(iii) any portion or part of any item described in clause (i) or (ii);

This law was drafted to give visual artists protection for the moral rights of paternity and integrity, but look carefully at the last paragraph quoted from Section 106A; the work has to be "of recognized stature." That phrase has never been defined. It therefore remains for a brave artist to come forward and invoke this pristine law that has never been used to protect any artist's rights.

It is interesting that the right of integrity to keep commercials in a satellite broadcast is protected by Title 17, United States Code, Section 119.

(4) Willful alterations.—

Notwithstanding the provisions of paragraphs (1) and (2), the secondary transmission to the public by a satellite carrier of a performance or display of a work embodied in a primary transmission made by a superstation or a network station is actionable as an act of infringement under section 501, and is fully subject to the remedies provided by sections 502 through 506 and sections 509 and 510, if the content of the particular program in which the performance or display is embodied, or any commercial advertising or station announcement transmitted by the primary transmitter during, or immediately before or after, the transmission of such program, is in any way willfully altered by the satellite carrier through changes, deletions, or additions, or is combined with programming from any other broadcast signal.

Under the copyright law, a satellite carrier can be criminally prosecuted if it does not transmit exactly what the broadcaster sent without alteration.

For murals created after June 1, 1991, there is some protection offered by Title 17, United States Code, Section 113, but the artist has some statutory formalities to follow in order to get it.

(d)(1) In a case in which—

(A) a work of visual art has been incorporated in or made part of a building in such a way that removing the work from the building will cause the destruction, distortion, mutilation, or other modification of the work as described in section 106A(a)(3), and

(B) the author consented to the installation of the work in the building either before the effective date set forth in section 610(a) of the Visual Artists Rights Act of 1990, or in a written instrument executed on or after such effective date that is signed by the owner of the building and the author and that specifies that installation of the work may subject the work to destruction, distortion, mutilation, or other modification, by reason of its removal, then the rights conferred by paragraphs (2) and (3) of section 106A(a) shall not apply.

(2) If the owner of a building wishes to remove a work of visual art which is a part of such building and which can be removed from the building without the destruction, distortion, mutilation, or other modification of the work as described in section 106A(a)(3), the author's rights under paragraphs (2) and (3) of section 106A(a) shall apply unless—

(A) the owner has made a diligent, good faith attempt without success to notify the author of the owner's intended action affecting the work of visual art, or

(B) the owner did provide such notice in writing and the person so notified failed, within 90 days after receiving such notice, either to remove the work or to pay for its removal.

In other words, if the artist keeps a current address in the office of the Register of Copyrights and does not sign an agreement with the building owner allowing the work to be altered or destroyed, the artist has the right to preserve and remove the work at his or her own expense within 90 days of the building owner's notice.

Notwithstanding the existence of legal protection for the "moral and material" rights of creative people, it must be noted that as a practical matter, this protection can be hard to get. Although there may be a legal provision which applies to a situation, there is no guarantee that the provision will be applied or followed.

Monterey Pop

In 1967 an artist named Tom Wilkes created all the artwork and posters for the Monterey International Pop Music Festival. His agreement was that he would retain ownership of all the artwork from the Festival. As required by the copyright statute, the artist placed a copyright notice—with his name—on all published work. Some years later he registered his copyright with the U.S. Copyright Office and received a copyright certificate.

In 1992, the 25th anniversary of the Festival, a record company released a compilation album featuring the music from the festival and using Wilkes' artwork on the cover and inside the album. The artist filed a lawsuit, claiming the violation of his copyright. The record company claimed it did not need the artist's permission to use the artwork.

In spite of the artist's fulfillment of every requirement under the copyright law to register and protect his artwork, the federal court agreed with the record company. It not only tossed the case out, but ordered the artist to pay almost $10,000.00 in attorneys fees to the record company.[58]

10

Trademark Law

Another, and sometimes more effective, area of protection for intellectual property is found in the law of trademark in Title 15, United States Code, Section 1125, also known as the Lanham Act.

> 1125.—False designations of origin, false descriptions, and dilution forbidden
>
> (a) Civil action
>
> (1) Any person who, on or in connection with any goods or services, or any container for goods, uses in commerce any word, term, name, symbol, or device, or any combination thereof, or any false designation of origin, false or misleading description of fact, or false or misleading representation of fact, which—
>
> (A) is likely to cause confusion, or to cause mistake, or to deceive as to the affiliation, connection, or association of such person with another person, or as to the origin, sponsorship, or approval of his or her goods, services, or commercial activities by another person, or
>
> (B) in commercial advertising or promotion, misrepresents the nature, characteristics, qualities, or geographic origin of his or her or another person's goods, services, or commercial activities, shall be liable in a civil action by any person who believes that he or she is likely to be damaged by such act.

This statute usually provides protection for commercial brand names, but it was one of the laws that was listed as protecting artists when Congress was considering the Berne treaty. It has been used effectively to provide damages to artists whose faces, names, and styles have been used in advertising products without their permission.

For example, the creator of the comic strip "Mutt and Jeff," Harry C. Fisher, had registered a trademark in his characters. When the newspaper that printed the comic strip tried to fight Fisher's switch to a syndicate and other newspapers, Fisher's trademark protected his rights. The court recognized that the public was entitled to receive and enjoy the humor of the author and the skill of the artist to which it had become accustomed.[59]

The Lanham Act, which includes claims of false advertising, could also arguably be used to protect an artist's right of integrity. Once a work has been altered, it is no longer the same work. Thus an advertisement announcing an upcoming broadcast of "The Sound of Music" on network television would be false and misleading if the version of the film aired was cut by one third to make room for commercials and interrupted by commercials. In this case, the film shown would not be the film that was created. It would be more truthful to advertise the broadcast of "pieces of The Sound of Music."

11

Contract Law

General Contract

The Monty Python lawsuit was based upon several grounds—including trademark law, as mentioned above—moral rights law and contract law. The court ruled in favor of the artists under the theory of contract law because the artists' contract with the British Broadcasting Company (BBC) prohibited making changes to the shows without the artists' consent and input. The trademark and moral rights violations were not ruled upon by the court, although the court's opinion goes to great lengths to explain and exalt moral rights.

Contractual provisions are the most secure manner in which an artist can protect his or her moral rights in the current American judicial climate. The primary drawback to this type of protection is the reality that the vast majority of artists have virtually no bargaining power when engaging in an art business transaction. The purchaser usually presents the artist with a "take it or leave it" proposition that requires the artist to give up artistic control over the work. Most artists who wish to make a living from their art cannot afford to refuse.

Work for Hire/Commissioned Works

When an artist is hired to create a work, there will be a contract regarding the rights of the respective parties in the work once it has been created. Except in the case of a fine art commission, the contract will be what is known as a "work for hire" or "work made for hire" contract. Every artist who has worked for an entertainment, news, publishing or software company has signed a work for hire contract. This contract gives the hiring party all rights to the finished work. It is normally used for collaborative works—works created from the contributions of many different artists—so that the party making the work will have complete ownership and control over the finished work. The artist's only right in a work for hire arrangement is to get paid, and often the payment reflects the nature of the artist's surrender of all rights by being higher.

The work for hire contract will not apply when a work has already been created by the artist and another party simply wishes to buy, or license it. In that case, for a party to get any rights in the work the artist will have to license or assign the rights to the purchaser, as discussed in the Copyright Law section above. The distinction is an important one, because a work for hire type surrender of all rights is permanent, but a "grant" of rights is not, as will be explained below.

The copyright act specifically defined the types of works that qualify under the law as works for hire at Title 17, United States Code, Section 101.

> A "work made for hire" is—
> (1) a work prepared by an employee within the scope of his or her employment; or
> (2) a work specially ordered or commissioned for use as a contribution to a collective work, as a part of a motion picture or other audiovisual work, as a translation, as a supplementary work, as a compilation, as an instructional text, as a test, as answer material for a test, or as an atlas, if the parties expressly agree in a written instrument signed by them that the work shall be considered a work made for hire. For the purpose of the foregoing sentence, a "supplementary work" is a work prepared for publication as a secondary adjunct to a work by another author for the purpose of introducing, concluding, illustrating, explaining, revising, commenting upon, or assisting in the use of the other work, such as forewords, afterwords, pictorial illustrations, maps, charts, tables, editorial notes, musical arrangements, answer material for tests, bibliographies, appendixes, and indexes, and an "instructional text"

is a literary, pictorial, or graphic work prepared for publication and with the purpose of use in systematic instructional activities.

In order for a work to be considered a work made for hire, the requirements of the law must be met precisely. It is important to note the requirement of a written contract. If an artist who is not an employee of the hiring party is hired to create a work which falls within the definition of a work made for hire, it will not be considered a work for hire if the artist did not sign a work for hire contract. On the other hand, if the work the artist is being hired to create does not fall within any of the above categories, then even if the artist signed a work for hire contract, the work is not a work made for hire. A contract that does not qualify as a work for hire contract will be regarded, legally, as an assignment, or grant of rights by the artist.

Any assignment or grant of rights by an artist which does not qualify as a work made for hire can be terminated by the artist or the artist's heirs 35 years after it is made as provided in Title 17, United States Code, Section 203.

> (3) Termination of the grant may be effected at any time during a period of five years beginning at the end of thirty-five years from the date of execution of the grant; or, if the grant covers the right of publication of the work, the period begins at the end of thirty-five years from the date of publication of the work under the grant or at the end of forty years from the date of execution of the grant, whichever term ends earlier.
>
> (4) The termination shall be effected by serving an advance notice in writing, signed by the number and proportion of owners of termination interests required under clauses (1) and (2) of this subsection, or by their duly authorized agents, upon the grantee or the grantee's successor in title.

A work for hire contract is not used when an artist is commissioned to create a work of fine art, although the parties will usually sign a contract. Even when the hiring party has the right to approve the design of the work before it is created or makes suggestions regarding changes to the work as it is being created, the artist is regarded as the creator and owner of all rights to the finished work. The hiring party merely owns physical possession of the work.

12

Other Legal Protection Available to Artists

Right of Publicity

In other countries, a violation of an artist's moral rights is treated as a violation of the artist's person. In the United States, the areas of law that address injury to the artist's person are most frequently the right of publicity, libel and slander, and the right of privacy.

Midler v. Ford

In 1985 Ford Motor Company, through its advertising agency, launched an advertising campaign to sell the new Lincoln Mercury cars by using popular songs. The advertising agency approached Bette Midler and asked her to sing a song she had popularized: "Do You Want to Dance." The artist stated that she was not interested in doing any commercials, so the agency hired a former backup singer for Midler and asked her to record the song, sounding as much as possible like Bette Midler. When the commercials ran, the general public thought the song was being sung by Bette Midler, creating an implication that the famous artist endorsed the automobile. Midler successfully sued both Ford and the advertising agency on the grounds that they had violated her right of publicity. In ruling for the artist, the court stated that the singer manifests herself in the song and that to impersonate her voice is to pirate her identity.[60]

Although everyone has the right to protect their name and likeness from being used in advertising without their permission, most people never have to worry about that. Thus the right of publicity is a claim usually reserved for the famous artist whose name, face, and particular talent are recognized as marketable.

Defamation, Libel and Slander

One of the more specific rights under the four broad categories of moral rights is the right to respond to excessive or unjust criticism. This right is directed at protecting the artist's reputation, but it has the added benefit of allowing an artist to exert some damage control over his or her commercial viability. The laws of libel and slander work in exactly the same way, except that, where criticism is protected as free speech by the Constitution, libel and slander are regarded as outright lies that deserve no protection. The requirements for libel (printed material) and slander (spoken material) are that the material being stated or printed is negative, untrue, and has an actual effect on the person's reputation.

An artist whose lifestyle has been misrepresented could find his or her reputation affected and would thus have an action for libel or slander. For example, *The National Enquirer* tabloid printed a story that Carol Burnett was seen in public at a party, drunk and disorderly. The artist, who was not a big drinker and whose fans are primarily seen as the "family oriented" mainstream audience, sued the paper and won damages for libel.

Right of Privacy

The right of privacy for an artist is closely related to the moral right of exhibition. It has been effectively used to prevent an artist's or a famous person's unpublished letters from being made public and possibly could have been useful in the example below, if the artist had wanted to incur the expense of litigation.

Garfield

The creator of the cartoon "Garfield", Jim Davis, has always held very strict control over all aspects of his work. One day he was approached by a New York art gallery, asking him to sign some "Garfield" drawings and animation cells. Davis was surprised and curious about where this gallery had obtained his artwork. He went there. When Davis saw what he was being asked to autograph, he immediately recognized drawings and cells which had been discarded. Someone had taken the artwork out of the trash dumpster at the animation studio where "Garfield" was drawn and had sold them to the gallery. Because it is not illegal to take someone's discards, Davis could not ask for them back. Now the artist holds very tight control over his trash, too.[61]

Common Law/Civil Law

One method our legal system has used to protect rights emanating from the natural law, but which are not actually statutes on the books, is to recognize them as part of the "common law."[62] That way, a court of law can address a person's rights even when a legislature has not gotten around to enacting a law on the subject. When a court is doing this, it is taking on the role of a court "in equity," concerning itself with what is fair and just. All courts are courts of equity, although it has at times been hard to recognize it.

Under the common law, artists enjoyed certain protections for their works, which were not provided in the copyright statutes, by virtue of a recognized doctrine called "common law copyright." In this way, artists sometimes were able to exert additional protection over their works.

Movie Crazy

In 1947 the silent film star Harold Lloyd sued Universal Pictures because they had taken 57 short comedy scenes from Lloyd's film, "Movie Crazy," and put them into a Universal picture called "So's

Your Uncle." The studio tried to defend itself by arguing that the comic scenes were not specifically mentioned in the copyright law as something the law protected. The court found that the letter of the law was merely worded for the convenience of the copyright office, for administrative purposes, and that certainly the creative work, as well as the earning potential of that work, was protected by the copyright law. The artist won.[63]

Effective January 1, 1978, Congress enacted a completely revamped Copyright Act, specifically stating that there would no longer exist anything called a common law copyright. The officially stated purpose of the law was to make copyright protection more comprehensive, understandable, and simple. In reality, it created specific bureaucratic requirements that an artist must fulfill in order to prevent someone from stealing his or her work. Under the current system, if the artist has failed to complete all the correct paperwork at the correct time, the artist has no protection whatsoever for the work.[64]

Again, the common law is a term meant to describe rights that exist independent of legislative statutes. A statute claiming that people have no rights other than those specifically stated in the statute is ridiculously authoritarian. Legislators are fallible human beings who cannot possibly recite each and every conceivable right a person may have and make a statute for it. There is no reason to give them that burden. The common law and equity fill in the gaps quite nicely. If this language in the copyright act were challenged under the right set of facts, a court of law would have to agree.

Unfair Competition

A broad area of common law trademark protection, as well as statutory protection under the law in most states, is unfair competition. Like trademark law, it addresses the deception of the public in being told that either the originator of the product or the product itself is something other than what it really is. It also addresses unfair business practices such as large businesses selling items below cost in order to drive smaller competitors out of business.

Artists have had inconsistent results using the theory of unfair competition to protect the commercial value of their work. In 1962 Bert Lahr successfully brought an action for unfair competition against a chemical company for imitating his voice through a cartoon duck in an advertising campaign.[65] In 1970 Nancy Sinatra sued a tire manufacturer and their advertising agency based on their use of "These Boots Are Made for Walkin'," with a sound and look alike. The court said that the activities did not constitute unfair competition, and Sinatra lost her case.[66] Incidentally, the advertising agency in that case was the same agency as in *Midler v. Ford*, above.

Mutt and Jeff

In 1921 the creator of the popular comic strip "Mutt and Jeff," switched to a syndicate for the marketing of his comic strip to various newspapers, rather than the one New York newspaper that had printed it for six years. The former newspaper, however, hired artists to imitate the comic strip and began to print an imitation "Mutt and Jeff" in its paper. The artist, Harry C. Fisher, had to bring a court action to stop it. In finding for the artist, the court recognized that Fisher invented the characters and that his "genius" pervaded everything about them. Selling inferior imitations was held to be an unfair appropriation of the artist's skill and the fame he had acquired through his art.[67]

Property Law

The rights of publicity regarding a deceased person are recognized as property rights, and under the common law, appropriation of another's identity is a violation of a property right.

Smokin'

In 1974 a cigarette company ran a television advertisement featuring a photograph of a racing car. In the photograph, the car was slightly altered and the face of Lothar Motschenbacher, a famous driver who was seated in the car in the photo, was not visible. The public correctly recognized the car as Motschenbacher's, and from that inferred both that he was in the car and that he endorsed the product. The court found that the cigarette company had violated the proprietary interest the race car driver had in his own identity.[68]

13

Public Opinion

The power of public opinion should not be underestimated when it comes to the protection of art and artists, because it is the public who ultimately finances all artistic business enterprise. For example, the passage of the law protecting public murals was motivated by public opinion. People were dismayed that public murals that touched their lives everyday and had become a part of them could be arbitrarily painted over. In order to address this concern, the law protecting murals was passed.

The Right Stuff

A couple of guys no one ever heard of drew a comic strip for fun and sold it in 1938 for $10.00 per page: $130.00 total. At the time, they thought they had made a pretty good deal. The name of that comic strip is "Superman," and it is a billion-dollar industry. It became publicly known some years ago that the original creators of Superman weren't getting any money from it and the modern owners of Superman were shamed into giving them a small annual salary of $10,000.00 apiece.

Public opinion is more powerful than any law ever enacted with regard to art. When the law won't protect art, it is up to the public to use its consumer power to insist on original, unedited versions of the art they enjoy and to refrain from buying, paying to see, listening to, or watching works that have been altered.

For example, most people do not know that Blockbuster Video edits scenes or images out of films that it does not feel are appropriate for a general audience. People think they are renting a copy of a feature film, when in reality a faceless entity has arbitrarily decided that certain parts of it should be removed. If the public showed its disapproval of this activity by not renting from Blockbuster, the company would have no choice but to stop this practice.

The most likely reason Charles Dickens was able to get publishing contracts with American publishers after years of piracy was that he physically came to this country and publishers feared he might ask people not to buy the unauthorized copies. Letting the public know what is going on is a very effective tool for an artist.

I read an interview with a Pulitzer-prize winning author whose book was being made into a television movie. He said, "I didn't have anything to do with this movie, not even the commas." That told me that the producers had made a lot of changes to the author's story, and he wasn't very happy about it. I watched the movie and it was awful. The worst part was the end where the movie introduced a new character to try to tie the rambling story together. After that experience, I let the artist be my guide.

If an artist doesn't like what is being done with his or her creation, there's probably a valid reason. If artists can make the public aware of the changes to their works and that they disapprove, the public will have the opportunity to avoid the *libri mendosi*. Most entertainment contracts prohibit an artist from openly criticizing a work, so an artist who truly objects has to be creative.

Another area where public knowledge is important is to help protect the artist from theft or piracy, formerly known as "plagiarism." Attitudes toward plagiarism have changed since Ancient Greece. "Plagiarism," as a term was used in our legal system until it was replaced by the word "infringement."

An analysis of the change in usage from the word "plagiarism" to the word "infringement" is given by Streibich:

Plagiarism is now an integral part of our law of copyright, yet the term is sometimes used interchangeably with 'infringement' to cloud the moral stigma of the harsh indictment and connotation of the word 'plagiarism.' An interesting observation was made on this point by Leonard Feist, Executive Vice President of the National Music Publishers Association. 'In our contemporary society, plagiarism is a crime upon which society frowns. Copyright infringement, however, is something like speeding. It's considered by many to be quite all right as long as you don't get caught.'[69]

Ideas are not protected by any laws, and a good idea can be worth a lot of money. Therefore, the more familiar people are with an artist's work, the less likely someone will be able to take that work and sell it as their own.

14

The Future

Use of Copyright Rights

With advances in technology, created works are distributed, reproduced, and even altered easily and with less expense. The question has come up in recent years as to whether new laws need to be passed, or whether current laws need to be revised to address new technologies and the Internet.

The answer is "No." The current system of laws protecting products of the mind apply to new technologies and the Internet in the exact same way they apply to earlier means of expression. That is, unauthorized copying, distribution, and sale of created works—in any medium—can be addressed by the current framework of laws in place and by the Berne Treaty.

That is not to say that the policymakers stationed in Washington, D.C. are not arguing for change. The sale of created works, especially from the entertainment industry, is generating more and more and more revenue all the time, and with this money comes the power to influence lawmakers and judicial mindsets. The people now in control of policy are concerned only with profits and they purport to speak for artists, claiming that they, too, are concerned only with getting paid. This argument sidesteps the artist's relationship with his or her work, and is simply untrue. For example, after Jonathan Winters retired from television, he would perform comedy in his local market. A family member asked him why he would rather perform for a few people for free than in an auditorium for many people and get paid thousands of dollars. His answer was that, in the market, he could perform comedy on his own terms.

The direction in which the talking heads in Washington D.C. seek to push copyright is toward a system of compulsory licensing like that now in place for music. In copyright, the creator of music does not have the right to authorize performances of the composition. Anyone can perform the music, as long as they pay a licensing fee to the copyright owner, who is usually not the composer. The compulsory licensing system is in direct conflict with the Berne Treaty, as it prevents the composer or lyricist from objecting to the manner in which the composition is being used. "Look What They Done to My Song, Ma."

In a book called *Copyright's Highway,* the book's author made the irresponsible prediction that in the future all created works would be included in a sort of "celestial jukebox," and that anyone could have access to the works they want just by putting in the required fee. Certainly new technologies make it easier to restore, protect, and store all sorts of created works, and private interests claiming to represent consumers tout greater access to created works. However, initiating a compulsory licensing system for all created works would represent a return to the monopoly and censorship that characterized intellectual property laws at the end of the Dark Ages.

Entertainment companies are merging into huge multimedia conglomerates, concentrating the means of production, distribution, and exhibition into fewer and fewer hands. There are fewer people deciding what the public sees, leading to less diversity and less controversy. The avenues of marketing created works—the key to public access—also fall under the umbrella of the multimedia concerns. Thus anyone outside the umbrella trying to gain access to the marketing stream or to the modes of exhibition would have to have a disproportionate amount of money to buy such access. The result would be a disaster for the free exchange of ideas.

With compulsory licensing, the creator's only rights would be to receive a fee. One commentator suggested that the artist's role would be reduced to that of a mere creditor[70], separated completely from the work they had created and which bears their name. The act of creating would lose all meaning, as shown by the following example.

In a familiar scene from a television commercial, a United States Marine Corps Drill Sergeant is berating a group of recruits in front of their barracks. Suddenly, the drill sergeant is approached by a superior officer, who is apparently looking for a misplaced six-pack of beer. The officer turns out to be John Wayne, a famous actor who died long before the commercial was ever made. It is immediately clear that John Wayne's face, body, and performance from a feature film has been digitally reproduced and inserted into a beer commercial. It is also clear that, since he is deceased, John Wayne could not have given his permission to be shown in the advertisement.

This type of art mauling is already being carried out in this country and it is perfectly allowed under the rubric of copyright law, because the copyright owner of the feature film received a payment for use of the film clip. In another example, an online publisher touts its technology-based content printing service, which allows its customers to draw chapters from various books and put them together into a "new" book tailored to the user's needs or desires.

It is the position of those who are lobbying for change in the copyright laws that such a system would be beneficial to the creative environment. In reality, it would simply allow entertainment leviathans to control more forms of creative expression and charge consumers for content that they may now access for free, such as Internet radio.

In addition, in direct conflict with the Constitutional mandate to "promote science and the useful arts," compulsory licensing would have the effect of discouraging creation in three ways:

1) Fewer people will be buying created works to sell to the public, creating fewer opportunities for artists. With greater control over the means of exhibiting and marketing works, large interests can edge out competition from artists whose work they did not buy, but who try to promote themselves.

2) Artists won't want to watch their works get chopped up and mismatched with the works of other artists. Works of art have a message, and that message would be destroyed if the work were to be torn apart. Paying an artist a fee for the right to do this won't make the creator feel any better to watch his or her creation, the child of his or her self, being used to communicate someone else's message. The artists' incentive to create would be squashed by the ease of replication of their works by "freeloaders."[71]

3) People will use other people's works to try to create "new" works without the benefit of the blank canvas. Such creations will not be original or new in any sense, and they could have the effect of creating distaste in the public for the original artwork, thereby harming the original artist's market and reputation undeservedly.

Many legal scholars predict a bleak future for artists' rights in the face of such powerful special interests. Although I have seen these phenomena and experienced the futility of one artist taking on an entertainment powerhouse in court, I do not believe the future needs to be so dark. A careful look at the progressing history of artists' rights laws in this country and our increasing recognition of the effort of creation shows that, legally, the protection for artists is growing, not receding.

We have finally joined the Berne Union. Powerful special interests could not keep this country out of it forever, and they cannot prevent enforcement of it forever. It is, after all, based on the inalienable Rights of Man, and the United States of America was the first voice to articulate those rights to the rest of the world.

Term of Copyright

In the spirit of the Statute of Anne, the first copyright act passed in the United States placed a limit of 14 years on the exclusive rights of a creator over their works. Since then, Congress has extended the term for copyright protection many times. In 1998, copyright was extended an additional 20 years, bringing the copyright term to 95 years. This is completely consistent with the Berne Treaty's extensive protection that regards an artist's rights as perpetual. In a 2003 decision, the United States Supreme Court upheld the constitutionality of the long copyright protection allowed under the current law. This decision was a nod toward greater protection for artists, and yet another step toward full United States compliance with the Berne Treaty.

There is, however, an incongruity between the natural law concept of the perpetual nature of artistic rights and the monopoly and censorship that results from a copyright owner having 95 years of exclusive control over thousands of works which they may or may not decide to share with the public. That is why to some, the recent Supreme Court decision resembles the 18th century case of *Millar v. Taylor,* discussed in Chapter 1, wherein the House of Lords upheld the printing monopoly of the Stationers' Company in the name of the perpetual nature of an artist's natural rights.

An example of this problem that bears a touch of urgency is in the area of film preservation. Thousands of films are disintegrating into ashes everyday, due to nitrate decomposition and other factors. The owners of the copyrights to those films have exclusive control over those films, not only with regard to their storage, but also with regard to whether those films will be restored and preserved. Anyone who would want to view, exhibit, or even restore any of these films must have the copyright owner's permission.

Under the Berne Treaty, a failure to address this problem would violate the moral right of integrity in the works. Artists or their heirs have the right to object to the alteration, mutilation, or destruction of their works, even if the destruction is due simply to the inaction of the copyright owner. The heirs of Buster Keaton, for example, have the right, under the Berne Treaty, to object to a copyright owner's allowing his films to sit in a vault and rot, thus forcing the owner to either restore the films, or release them to someone else who will. This is a course of action that is available now and could be invoked more and more in the future as other types of works begin to disintegrate with the passage of time, and decisions are made as to which works will be transferred into new media.

It bears noting that in the author's conversations with John Merryman, a well-known art law expert, he expressed a belief that the destruction of an artist's work was also a violation of the artist's moral right to a resale royalty. Once the work no longer exists, it can no longer generate royalties for the artist. In addition, works not being made available to the public do not create revenue. Copyright owners use their libraries of copyrights as collateral when borrowing money to finance new projects. The artist entitled to royalties receives no benefit from this practice.

The economic effect of the destruction, or the refusal to distribute art also has remedies in other areas of American law, such as unfair competition, contract, and property. Thus if a copyright owner has the right to invoke the principles of artists' rights to protect its economic interests, the artists must also have that right.

A possible solution which balances the economic interests of all parties would be to adapt the custom in use in the publishing industry to all areas of art. In publishing, when a book goes out of print the author has the right to request that it be put back into print by the publisher. If the publisher doesn't comply, all rights return to the author, who may then try to re-publish the book. Thus in the case of a film, any of the artists who created the film and who are entitled to royalties, or their heirs, could demand that their work be distributed, and if the copyright owner doesn't comply the artists could take back the film and try to exhibit or distribute it on their own. A system of this nature would address the concerns of perpetuity, monopoly, and public access to the works.

PART III

What Can Be Done

15

The Special Nature of Art

Why should everyone care about the legal rights of artists? To understand this, it is necessary to look at what happens when a work of art is allowed to communicate with people in its original form.

At the beginning of the 20th century, America was undergoing an industrial revolution. Commerce was controlled by a few captains of industry while the influx of immigrants provided a steady supply of labor. One author, Upton Sinclair, wrote a novel about the plight of an immigrant family struggling against poverty while working in the meatpacking industry of Chicago. The author hoped that *The Jungle* would instigate a worker's revolt and pave the way for socialism. It did inspire a revolution, but not as the author planned. The public was outraged at the unsanitary conditions in the meatpacking plants, which the novel described in graphic detail. As a result, the federal government established health standards for food processing and handling.

In the 1930's, millions of impoverished farmers were displaced from their farms—the only homes they and their parents had ever known—and forced to look for a new home and a new livelihood among strangers in strange surroundings. As documented in John Steinbeck's *The Grapes of Wrath*, the farm families lived in a constant, desperate struggle for survival. The struggle claimed the lives of so many through the slow, painful effects of starvation.

In 1936 a photographer named Dorothea Lange was commissioned by the federal government to document the westward migration of the displaced farmers with her camera. She happened upon a woman and her three children alone on a small vacant lot. The pea crop, it seemed, had been destroyed by a flood, so there was nothing to pick, no wages to be earned. While the other migrants had moved on, this family had fashioned a shelter out of their car, the tires of which had been traded for the previous day's meal.

With their permission, Lange began photographing the woman and her children. Suddenly, the effects of everything these people had been through coalesced in a single moment and the photographer was there to capture it. In two days the now-famous photograph, "Migrant Mother, Nipomo, California," was on the front page of the *San Francisco Chronicle*, and the United States government rushed in to set up relief centers within the week. To this day, "Migrant Mother" is the most requested image in the Library of Congress catalogue.

In 1981, doctors in various cities noticed that people began to suffer from a strange illness which depressed their immune systems and made them vulnerable to diseases that normally did not pose any threat to healthy humans. With no ability to fight disease, the afflicted person would usually die within a relatively short time. The National Center for Disease Control knew about this strange new malady, but since most people who died of it were homosexual men, no funding would be committed to researching or fighting this strange virus, or even to educating people about it. Protests, rallies, and marches were staged to bring attention to this life-threatening condition, but they would often go ignored in the news media as not having a "general" interest.

Finally, the families of some of the deceased needed an outlet to express their grief. They decided to make a quilt. Each square of the quilt depicted a person who had died of AIDS. In 1987 the quilt was spread out on the ground in the National Mall in Washington, D.C., the scene of so many previous marches and vigils to raise AIDS awareness. The next morning, the AIDS Quilt was pictured on the front page of every major newspaper in the country and made its way into the evening news on television.

One simple work of art communicated more in one instant than thousands of voices speaking with conventional methods over several years. With the increase in public awareness came the long sought-after government health funding to educate against, fight, and prevent the spread of AIDS. The Quilt is not for sale. It has not been given a price-tag, but millions of people will attest that it has enormous value.[72]

As works of art—*The Jungle*, "Migrant Mother," and the AIDS Memorial Quilt—have done what so many other examples of creative expression do to us. They moved us. The ability of art to communicate is, in fact, the original source of its value, separate and apart from the sales price. Thus the value of a work of art can be perceived in two separate ways. One source of value is the communication value of the work—what it says to us. The other source of value is the market value—what someone will pay for it.

In 1993 a published study by the University of California at Irvine concluded that listening to Mozart's Sonata for 2 Pianos in D major increased the listener's scores on an Intelligence Quotient (I.Q.) test.[73] The resulting "Mozart effect" could not be explained by the scientists conducting the experiment, but there really is no need for an explanation. Through the barrier of time and physical mortality, the creative expression of one individual was perceived and understood by listeners in a completely different century. On some level, the music communicated with the test subjects and the test subjects themselves responded to the communication. The I.Q. test was simply the objective litmus paper where the response showed itself. The results showed that something in that creative expression was universal enough to last.

It is that something—that ability of art to communicate—that moral rights laws protect. The right to the protection of that communication is as much a human right as the protection of free radio broadcasts that are not generated or controlled by a ruling government.

16

Winning the Tug of War Over Art

As stated earlier, American laws and courts address that which is easier to define and to measure. They have previously been reluctant to recognize moral rights because moral rights have traditionally been viewed as the artist's rights of "personality." In the modern age, a more practical and effective method of recognizing moral rights would be realized by looking at what moral rights protect.

A work of art has two types of value, like the two sides of a coin. On one side is the artistic expression. The artwork communicates something that the artist is trying to express, and the person responding to it perceives it as "good." The perception of the work as "good" creates a demand to buy it. This brings up the other side of the coin: the market, or commercial value of the work, where a price tag is applied. American law does protect some commercial aspects of art, but just like a coin, the two sides cannot exist independently of each other. The communication value of a created work is every bit as important as its market value, and protecting moral rights protects both.

Artists keenly observe the world around them and struggle to express their observations faithfully, but they also need to eat. They must depend for their survival on the recognition of their abilities and the appreciation of their artistic work. It is the communication value of the artwork which provides these two essential elements of the artist's success—recognition and appreciation—and perceiving the work as good is what makes people want to buy the art in the first place. The communication value produces the artist's "reputation" as a talented artist and is therefore directly tied to the artist's livelihood. For that reason, the artist has an ongoing connection to the artwork, even after it has been sold.

This part of the artwork's value cannot be sold or transferred. The communication value of the artwork originates and remains with the artist. No matter who owns the art, two things will remain the same: the original expression, and the artist. Thus the artist has a vested commercial interest in making sure that what makes the work good is preserved and protected. This recognition of an artist's commercial interest in his or her work and reputation is definitely something American laws can protect.

The reason we do not have moral rights protection in this country is that powerful interests in the lucrative entertainment industry have fought very hard to keep moral rights laws from being passed and to keep courts from recognizing the moral rights doctrine. Their fear and their argument is the same: if artists have these rights, then they can interfere with our rights to market the properties we have spent so much money to either purchase or create. This fear, however, is as illogical as a phobia, when compared to the actual protection afforded by moral rights laws.

Such laws do not take control away from the copyright owners; they merely supplement and enhance the skeletal framework of American copyright laws. The relationship between the communication value and the market value of artistic expression are illustrated very well in the example below.

Bergerot

In 1969 a painter named Bergerot made a contract with an art dealer that, for a monthly salary of 1200 francs, the artist would sell to the art dealer all the work he produced. On average, the artist was delivering about 18 works per month to the dealer. As the artist's work became more popular, his salary eventually increased to

2500 francs—more than twice the original amount. Even so, a dispute arose between the artist and the art dealer. The dealer decided that since he had built the artist's fame, he could tear it down. He advertised bargain basement prices for works by Bergerot and glutted the market with marked-down paintings. As a result, prices on Bergerot's works plummeted.[74]

The artist was understandably upset and claimed his moral rights were violated, but they weren't. In fact, it was the art dealer who had created the market price of the works in the first place. Following a common practice used by art dealers at the time, he made gifts of Bergerot's paintings to art critics, reminding the critics that they had the power to increase the value of their gift paintings by their criticism. This is the effect an art critic can have on art. Although the critic purports to speak on the quality of a work of art, the critic's words can actually only affect the sales value and short term demand for the work. As Victor Hugo wrote in *Les Misérables*:

> It may be remarked in passing that success is an ugly thing. Men are deceived by its false resemblances to merit. ...Prosperity presupposes ability. Win a lottery-prize and you are a clever man. ...Be fortunate and you will be thought great. ...—all this is what men call genius, just as they call a painted face beauty and a richly attired figure majesty. They confound the brilliance of the firmament with the star-shaped footprints of a duck in the mud.

The court in Bergerot's case was not confused. It ruled against him. The artist clearly did not have any control over the art dealer's activities or what steps the art dealer took to market the art. Moral rights laws could not be invoked to place any restrictions whatsoever on the art dealer's marketing activities which did not interfere with the public's perception of the actual works.

Negative criticism of the film "The Color Purple" did not hurt its producer, Steven Spielberg, commercially, despite its personal sting. Sometimes works of art, such as films, may be critically acclaimed, but they do not enjoy commercial success. However, if they communicate well, they will last. For example, Disney's "Fantasia" was neither a critical nor a commercial success when it was first released, but it is now considered a classic. Modern fans have purchased millions of videos, and the film has been re-released in movie theatres to capacity audiences. It's modern popularity inspired a sequel—decades after the original.

Similarly, the original "Star Trek" television series lasted only three seasons until it was cancelled by the television network. At that time, it did not achieve the market value the television executives were after. However, the original series just won't go away, because it communicates well. It communicates volumes about American culture, and especially American culture at that point in time.

Market value and communication value are completely different aspects of a created work. Although they are related, protecting one type of value does not necessarily protect both. The American point-of-view is that if someone has acquired the rights to make money with the artwork, then that person is the best one to control or take care of it. This, as practical experience has shown, is simply untrue.

No Court Press

When famous American sculptor David Smith was killed in 1965, the pain he suffered from seeing the alterations to his artwork was in every obituary. Smith learned that the owner of one of his sculptures, called "17 h's", had altered it by stripping the paint from it. Having been told he had no legal remedy, Smith took his grievances to the media, writing open letters to various art publications, which were published. Ironically, an influencial art critic named Clement Greenberg was named as one of the executors of Smith's estate and, in his capacity as keeper of the artist's remaining works, he proceeded to alter them. It had been Greenberg's own criticism and influence which had elevated the market value of Smith's work and created the demand for it. Greenberg had consistently rated the unpainted sculptures as more valuable and of a higher artistic quality than the painted ones. Consequently, the critic removed the paint from the sculptures he controlled, as executor of the estate, in order to raise their sales price.[75]

The purpose of moral rights protection is to prevent the people who are only concerned with the market value of a work of art from interfering with its communication value. When looking for the communication value in a created work, it is essential to remember that an original artwork is the expression of something that comes from within, not without. The impact of the AIDS Memorial Quilt, for example, comes from the fact that it is an expression of emotion, not the result of an effort to create something to sell.

A legal recognition of the communication value of a work of art will create a balancing test that will protect the artist's commercial interest in his or her own reputation as much as it now protects a marketer's commercial activities with the work itself.

17

What Artists Can Do

The most effective guardian of an artist's legal and moral rights is the artist. In order to effectively protect themselves, artists need to be informed. For example, the creator of "My Big Fat Greek Wedding" pitched her screenplay all around Hollywood, but no one would agree to make the movie she wanted it to be. She knew enough about her business to know that a producer would likely change her story once she sold the rights. She simply refused to sell the rights to anyone unless they agreed to make the movie according to her vision. She turned her story into a stage play, and finally someone agreed to make the movie as she wanted it, with her as the star. The film was a commercial and critical success.

After only four years of acting in American films, Charlie Chaplin became recognized as a comedy genius. He started performing on the stage and knew every aspect of his craft. Over time, he also became increasingly frustrated with his lack of creative control over films in which he was regarded solely as an actor. In 1917, Chaplin left his lucrative studio job to become an independent filmmaker. The artist could then control every aspect of the film, from writing and directing to scoring and editing. One of his independent films, "The Kid," was more successful than any other film released up to that point except "Birth of a Nation."

Great things can happen when artists are allowed to communicate directly with an audience and take charge over their works. Some of the most popular books ever written have been self-published, including Upton Sinclair's *The Jungle* and Victor Hugo's *Les Misérables*.

Admittedly, it is hard for a starving artist to remain steadfast in the face of a large check, but there will always be a market—sometimes a bigger market—for the work as the artist wants it to be seen.

Knowledge is power. Artists who wish to make a living from their art must know everything about it. They must read their trade publications for information on pricing, trends, and legal and business developments. A good way to learn from the mistakes of others is to read, or view, the biographies of other artists. Artists can also pay attention to what is going on with regard to arts legislation and programs by reading the newspaper and watching C-SPAN or by allying themselves with a group that advocates artists rights. A list of arts organizations and websites is given in the back of this book.

Finally, be a citizen. Artists are taxpayers, too. Artists vote and have, believe it or not, the same access to lawmakers that special interest groups have. Ordinary people just don't spend as much time in front of their elected representatives as people paid to sit there do. The letters and telephone calls of voters do have an effect on a lawmaker's ideas, and when such calls and letters come in large numbers, that individual will definitely be moved to act in some way.

Conclusion

In 1776, the people who invented this country did something that no other humans on earth had dared try before. They risked their lives to declare that all human beings have rights, and those rights exist independent of any sovereign. The idea was so revolutionary, yet so natural, it could not help but change the world forever.

Laws reflect the society that passes them. Barbara Ringer observed that a nation's copyright laws lie at the roots of its culture and intellectual climate. It is clear from a comparison between the legal protection for artists in this country and that in other countries that our society is still in its early stages of development.

Founded upon the principles of natural law, the country moved quickly into a society based upon the "social contract," and for the most part, it has not progressed beyond that point. Once inalienable rights were first declared, more established cultures quickly and effectively set up a framework for protecting the creative expressions of their people. Such an understanding of the importance of artistic contribution is still finding its way here. As Supreme Court Justice Oliver Wendell Holmes, Jr. lamented, "We have not the regard for artists that is the glory of France."[76] There can be no doubt, however, that we will.

Art brings truths to us that we don't perceive anywhere else, except in nature. We all have a right to the quality of life offered to us by original works of creative expression in all forms, including those of nature. Protecting and respecting art and artists has no disadvantages, even for the handful of companies who now own and control most of what the public sees. The insecure motivation to monopolize and censor products of the mind just doesn't work anymore, and the modern world has no place for it, thank goodness. After all, the denial of the inalienable human rights of anyone in this, the birthplace of such rights, is simply…unacceptable.

Notes

1. Streibich, H. "The Moral Right of Ownership to Intellectual Property: Part I—From the Beginning to The Age of Printing," 7 Mem. St. U. L. Rev. 1, 1–2 (1975)
2. *Encyclopedia Britannica*, "Human Rights"
3. Streibich, Ibid. at 8
4. Putnam, G. H., *Authors and Their Public In Ancient Times*, (1967)
5. Id.
6. *Encyclopedia Britannica*, "Human Rights"
7. Streibich, Ibid. at 24
8. Streibich, Ibid. at 27
9. Streibich, H. "The Moral Right of Ownership to Intellectual Property: Part II-From the Age of Printing to the Future," 7 Mem. St. U. L. Rev. 45, 46 (1975)
10. Putnam, See note 4, above
11. Streibich—Part II at 47
12. Davis, I., "A Century of Copyright: The United Kingdom and the Berne Convention," 11 Col.—VLA J. Law and the Arts 33, 34 (1986)
13. Streibich—Part II at 47
14. *Encyclopedia Britannica*, "Human Rights"
15. Ricketson, S. "The Birth of the Berne Union," 11 Col.—VLA J. Law and the Arts 9 (1986)
16. Id. at 17
17. Id. at 18
18. Id. at 19
19. Sandison, H., "The Berne Convention and the Universal Copyright Convention: The American Experience," 11 Col.—VLA J. Law and the Arts 89 (1986)

20. Kase, F. *Copyright Thought in Continental Europe: Its Development, Legal Theories and Philosophy* (1967)
21. *Encyclopedia Britannica*, "Human Rights"
22. Id.
23. United Nations Declaration of Human Rights
24. World Intellectual Property Organization, *Guide to the Berne Convention*, pp.41–44
25. *Guille v. Colmant* (1967) Cour d'Appel, Paris, Gaz. Pal. 1967.1.17, reported in Sarraute, R. "Current Theory on the Moral Right of Authors and Artists Under French Law," 16 Am. J. Comp. L. 478–479 (1968)
26. "Christmas Unwrapped: The History of Christmas," ©1999 A&E Television Networks
27. *Banque de France v. Mers* (1937), Cour d'Appel, Paris, Dalloz Hebd. 1936, 256, reported in out of print translation of French moral rights textbook in author's possession
28. King, S., "Why I Was Bachman," foreword to *The Bachman Books*
29. Merryman, J. and Elsen, A., *Law, Ethics and the Visual Arts* (1979)
30. *Millet* (1911) Amm. I. 271 (Tribunal de la Seine), reported in Merryman, J. "The Refrigerator of Bernard Buffet," 27 Hastings L.J. 1023, 1029 (1976)
31. *Gilliam v. American Broadcasting Companies, Inc.* (1976) 538 F.2d 14
32. *Rigault v. Chaperot* (1938) Trib. civ., Seine, Sirey, 1938.2.57, reported in Out of Print, Ibid.
33. *Shostakovich v. Twentieth Century-Fox Film Corp.* (1948) 196 Misc. 67, 80 N.Y.S.2d 575
34. *DuPassage v. Val d'Osne* (1894) Trib. civ., Seine Annales 1895, 232, reported in Out of Print, Ibid.
35. *Sudre v. Commune de Baixas* (1936) D. P. III. 57 (Conseil d'Etat), reported in Merryman, Ibid. at 1034
36. Id. at 1034

37. *Felseneiland mit Sirenen* (1912) 79 Entscheidungen des Reichsgerichts in Zivilsachen [RGZ] 397, reported in Merryman, Ibid. at 1038

38. *L'Affaire Camoin* (1931) Cour d'Appel, Paris D.P.2.88, reported in Da Silva, R. "Artists Rights in France and the U.S.," 28 Bull. Copr. Soc'y 1 (1980)

39. *L'Affaire Rouault* (1949) Cour d'Appel, Paris, D.P.20, reported in Da Silva, Ibid. at 19

40. *L'Affaire Ferré* (1964) Cour d'Appel, Paris, D.1964.229, reported in Sarraute, Ibid. at 475

41. Katz, A. "The Doctrine of Moral Right and American Copyright Law—A Proposal," 24 S. Cal. L. Rev. 375 (1951)

42. Da Silva, Ibid. at 54

43. Katz, Ibid. at 386

44. Ricketson, Ibid. at 23

45. Ringer, B. "The Role of the United States in International Copyright—Past, Present and Future," 56 Georgetown L.J. 1050 (1953)

46. Sandison, Ibid. at 91

47. Id. at 92

48. Id. at 93

49. Ringer, Ibid. at 1058–1059

50. Katz, Ibid. at 387

51. *Gilliam*, above at note 31, 23

52. *Vargas v. Esquire* (1947) 164 F.2d 522

53. www.stephenking.com

54. *Big Seven Music v. Lennon* (1977) 554 F.2d 504

55. Longmuir, S. "The Americanization of Droit Moral in the California Art Preservation Act," 15 Jour. Int'l Law & Politics, 901 (1983)

56. *Crimi v. Rutgers Presbyterian Church* (1949) 194 Misc. 570, 89 N.Y.S.2d 813

57. *Los Angeles Lawyer Magazine*, Entertainment Law Issue, April, 1990

58. *Wilkes v. Rhino Records, Inc.* U.S.D.C. 95-0734 (Cal.), upheld on appeal to the United States Court of Appeal for the Ninth Circuit in an unpublished opinion

59. *Star Co. v. Wheeler Syndicate, Inc.* (1915) 91 Misc. 640; 155 N.Y.S. 782

60. *Midler v. Ford Motor Co.* (9th Cir. 1988) 849 F.2d 460

61. Story recited by producer of "Garfield" animated television series at a lecture given by the author

62. See discussion under Fledgling Copyright Law in Chapter 4

63. *Harold Lloyd Corporation v. Universal Pictures Co.* (1947) 162 F.2d 354

64. Da Silva, Ibid. at 38

65. *Lahr v. Adell Chemical Co.* (1st Cir. 1962) 300 F.2d 256

66. *Sinatra v. Goodyear tire & Rubber Co.* (9th Cir. 1970) 435 F.2d 711

67. *Fisher v. Star Co.* (1921) 231 N.Y. 414, 132 N.E. 133

68. Motschenbacher v. R.J. Reynolds Tobacco Co. (9th Cir. 1974) 498 F.2d 821

69. Streibich—Part I at 7

70. Koumantos, G., "The Future of the Berne Convention," 11 Col.—VLA J. Law and the Arts 225 (1986)

71. Kaplan, B., *An Unhurried View of Copyright* (1967)

72. More information on the AIDS Memorial Quilt can be found at www.aidsquilt.org

73. *Nature* magazine, October 14, 1993

74. *Martin-Calle v. Bergerot* (1969) D.S. Jur. 73 (Cass. civ. Ire.), reported in Merryman, Ibid. at 1023

75. Reported in Merryman, "The Refrigerator of Bernard Buffet," 27 Hastings L.J. 1023 (1976)

76. *Tyson and Brothers v. Banton* (1927) 273 U.S. 418

References

There are many organizations composed of attorneys who provide their services to artists. This is the most current list available at publication.

California Lawyers for the Arts (CLA)
Northern California
Fort Mason Center, C-255
San Francisco, CA 94123
(415) 775-7200

Southern California
1641 18th Street
Santa Monica, CA 90404
(310) 998-5590
www.calawyersforthearts.org

Colorado Lawyers for the Arts (CoLA)
PO Box 48148
Denver CO 80204
(303) 722-7994
www.coloradoartslawyers.org

Connecticut Volunteer Lawyers for the Arts (CTVLA)
Connecticut Commission on the Arts
One Financial Plaza
Hartford, CT 06103
(860) 566-4770
www.ctarts.org

Georgia Lawyers for the Arts (GLA)
675 Ponce De Leon Ave. NE
Atlanta, GA 30308-1829
(404) 873-3911
www.glarts.org

Lawyers for the Creative Arts (LCA)
213 West Institute Place, Suite 401
Chicago, Illinois 60610-3125
(312) 649-4111
www.law-arts.org

Louisiana Volunteer Lawyers for the Arts (LVLA)
c/o Arts Council of New Orleans
821 Gravier Street, Suite 600
New Orleans, Louisiana 70112
(504) 523-1465

Maine Lawyers and Accountants for the Arts
43 Pleasant Street
South Portland, ME 04106
(207) 799-9646

Maryland Lawyers for the Arts
218 West Saratoga St.
Baltimore, Maryland 21201
(410) 752-1633

Lawyers for the Arts/New Hampshire
New Hampshire Business Committee for the Arts (NHBCA)
One Granite Place
Concord, New Hampshire 03301
(603) 224-8300
www.nhbca.com

North Carolina Volunteer Lawyers for the Arts
P.O. Box 26513
Raleigh, North Carolina 27611-6513
(919) 95N-CVLA (956-2852)
www.ncvla.org

Philadelphia Volunteer Lawyers for the Arts (PVLA)
251 South 18th Street
Philadelphia, Pennsylvania 19103
(215) 545-3385
www.pvla.org

St. Louis Volunteer Lawyers and Accountants for the Arts
(SLVLAA)
6128 Delmar
St. Louis, Missouri 63112
(314) 863-6930
www.vlaa.org

Texas Accountants and Lawyers for the Arts (TALA)
1540 Sul Ross
Houston, TX 77006
(713) 526-4876
Toll Free: (800) 526-8252
www.talarts.org

Volunteer Lawyers for the Arts (VLA)
1 East 53rd St, 6th Floor
New York, NY 10022-4201
(212) 319-2787, ext. 1
www.vlany.org

Volunteer Lawyers for the Arts of Massachusetts, Inc.
249 A Street, Studio 14
Boston, Massachusetts 02210
(617) 350-7600
www.vlama.org

Washington Area Lawyers for the Arts (WALA)
1300 I Street N.W., Suite 700
Washington, DC 20005
(202) 289-4440
www.thewala.org

Washington Lawyers for the Arts
819 N. 49th #207
Seattle, WA 98103
(206)328-7053
www.wa-artlaw.org

Wisconsin Lawyers for the Arts
PO Box 1054
Madison, WI 53701-1054
(608) 255-8316
www.wisconsinarts.org

The following organizations provide assistance to artists in their various fields of endeavor.

The Academy of American Poets
588 Broadway, Suite 604
New York, NY 10012-3210
www.poets.org

Academy of Country Music
4100 West Alameda Avenue, Suite 208
Burbank, CA 91505-4151
www.acmcountry.com

Actors Equity Association
National Headquarters
165 West 46th Street
New York, NY 10036
www.actorsequity.org

The American Dance Guild, Inc.
P.O. Box 2006, Lenox Hill Station
New York, NY 10021
www.americandanceguild.org

American Federation of Musicians
New York Headquarters
1501 Broadway, Suite 600
New York, NY 10036

West Coast Office
3550 Wilshire Blvd., Suite 1900
Los Angeles, CA 90010
www.afm.org

American Federation of Television & Radio Artists
National Headquarters
260 Madison Avenue, 7th Floor
New York, NY 10016-2401
www.aftra.org

American Guild of Musical Artists
1430 Broadway, 14th Floor
New York, NY 10018
www.MusicalArtists.org

American Society of Cinematographers
1782 North Orange Drive
Hollywood, CA 90028
www.theasc.com

American Society of Composers, Authors & Publishers
ASCAP—New York
One Lincoln Plaza
New York, NY 10023

ASCAP—Los Angeles
7920 W. Sunset Boulevard, Third Floor
Los Angeles, CA 90046
www.ascap.com

American Society of Media Photographers, Inc.
150 North Second Street
Philadelphia, PA 19106
www.asmp.org

Cartoonists Association
113 University Place, 6th Floor
New York, New York 10003
www.cartoonistsassociation.com

Directors Guild of America
7920 Sunset Blvd.
Los Angeles, California 90046
www.dga.org

The Dramatists Guild of America, Inc.
1501 Broadway, Suite 701
New York, NY 10036
www.dramaguild.com

Graphic Artists Guild
90 John Street, Suite 403
New York, NY 10038-3202
www.gag.org

National Sculpture Society
237 Park Avenue
New York, NY 10017
www.nationalsculpture.org

National Writers Union
National Office
113 University Pl. 6th Fl.
New York, NY 10003
www.nwu.org

Romance Writers of America
16000 Stuebner Airline Rd. Suite 140
Spring, TX 77379
www.rwanational.org

Screen Actors Guild
National Contact Information
5757 Wilshire Blvd.
Los Angeles, CA 90036-3600
www.new.sag.org

Society of Children's Book Writers and Illustrators
8271 Beverly Blvd.
Los Angeles, CA 90048
www.scbwi.org

The Society of Composers & Lyricists
400 S. Beverly Drive, Suite 214
Beverly Hills, CA 90212
www.filmscore.org

Society of Stage Directors and Choreographers
1501 Broadway, Suite 1701
New York, NY 10036
www.ssdc.org

Women In Film
8857 W. Olympic Blvd., Ste. #201
Beverly Hills, CA 90211
www.wif.org

Writers Guild of America, West
7000 West Third Street
Los Angeles, CA 90048
www.wga.org

Writers Guild of America, East
555 West 57th Street, Suite 1230
New York, NY 10019.
www.wgaeast.org

The information available to artists on the Internet is virtually unlimited. For thousands of links to arts and arts support organizations as well as a wealth of resources for artists go to www.artlynx.org.

Index

About the Author

Amelia V. Vetrone is an attorney in Los Angeles who has worked as an advocate for artists for 15 years. Her most famous lawsuit involved determining the copyright ownership of the original drawings of "Beavis and Butthead," resulting in a precedent-setting decision and an appearance on Court TV.

Based on the belief that supporting the rights of creators nourishes the cultural fabric of society, the author founded Vetrone Foundation for the Arts in 1991 as a resource for artists. She also has supported the programs of other arts organizations, such as the Artists Rights Foundation and California Lawyers for the Arts, as a volunteer panelist, mediator and writer.

The author has also written for the legal profession in the areas of art, copyright, and trademark in legal reference guides published by Matthew Bender & Co. as well as several articles in periodicals such as the *Los Angeles Daily Journal, House Counsel, Cyber, Esq.* and *California Law Business.*

For information about this book or its author please write:

TRUFFLEHUNTERS, INC.
P.O. Box 3191
South Pasadena, California 91031

0-595-29683-1